Buffalo Bill
on the Silver Screen

THE WILLIAM F. CODY SERIES
ON THE HISTORY AND CULTURE
OF THE AMERICAN WEST

Buffalo Bill on the Silver Screen

The Films of William F. Cody

Sandra K. Sagala

University of Oklahoma Press : Norman

Library of Congress Cataloging-in-Publication Data

Sagala, Sandra K.
    Buffalo Bill on the silver screen : the films of William F. Cody / Sandra K.
Sagala.
        pages   cm. — (The William F. Cody Series on the History and Culture
of the American West ; 1)
    Includes bibliographical references and index.
    ISBN 978-0-8061-4361-3 (hardcover : alk. paper) 1. Buffalo Bill, 1846–1917.
2. Pioneers–West (U.S.)—Biography. 3. Entertainers—United States—
Biography. 4. Actors—United States—Biography. 5. Motion picture producers
and directors—United States—Biography. 6. Documentary films—United
States—History and criticism. 7. Motion picture industry—United States—
History—20th century. 8. Buffalo Bill, 1846–1917—In motion pictures.
I. Title.
    F594.B94S35 2013
    978'.02092—dc23
    [B]

                                                                    2012039450

Buffalo Bill on the Silver Screen: The Films of William F. Cody is Volume 1
in The William F. Cody Series on the History and Culture of the American West.

The paper in this book meets the guidelines for permanence and durability
of the Committee on Production Guidelines for Book Longevity of the
Council on Library Resources, Inc. ∞

1 2 3 4 5 6 7 8 9 10

For
Joseph G. Rosa

Contents

Illustrations

Series Editors' Foreword

The William F. Cody Series on the History and Culture of the American West, a collaboration between the University of Oklahoma Press and The Papers of William F. Cody at the Buffalo Bill Center of the West, encourages interdisciplinary scholarship on the regional, national, and international influence of William F. Cody's life and enterprises, including Buffalo Bill's Wild West. Cody's extraordinary rise as impresario of one of the most popular traveling exhibitions in entertainment history reflects the forces shaping American national consciousness in the late nineteenth and early twentieth centuries. Encompassing an era that began with U.S. attempts to secure a continental empire and ended with the nation's emergence onto the global stage in the years leading up to World War I, the works appearing in this series will generate new perspectives on the dramatically changing world that Cody inhabited. Although the man and his international legacy have long been subjects of scholarly and popular interest, the scholarship in this series will benefit from the ever-growing documentary record detailing the material

history and cultural impact of the Buffalo Bill phenomenon.
An expanding archive, along with new research methodologies
and critical perspectives, will continue to shape our understanding of the American West.

The Papers of William F. Cody endeavors to document the
historic evolution and idealization of the American West through
the eyes of William F. "Buffalo Bill" Cody in both digital and
print publications. This book series is supplemented by The
William F. Cody Archive (www.codyarchive.org), a scholarly digital
archive that provides researchers and online visitors a rich array
of primary materials documenting Cody's interactions with individuals ranging from statesmen and royalty to noted military
and literary figures who reflect his Wild West celebrity. In addition, materials from his lesser-known roles as a community
founder, businessman, rancher, and investor speak to the larger
political, economic, and environmental policies affecting western
development during his lifetime.

Cody Archive provides access to a wide range of archival
material drawn from the resources of public and private collections from across the United States and Europe: memoirs and
autobiographies; correspondence; business records; published
and unpublished writings; photographs; video and audio recordings; promotional and Wild West materials; and newspaper and
magazine articles. All documents are digitized and transcribed
from original sources, encoded and edited—many enhanced
with annotations and translations—to provide metadata that
allows for associations across the archive and interoperability
with digital objects from other repositories. Each title in The
William F. Cody Series on the History and Culture of the American West will have a companion digital module, available at the
Cody Studies website (www.codystudies.org), compiled and annotated in cooperation with the book's author and including links
to digital materials relevant to the publication's theme. Readers

with electronic access will be able to explore the available sources for each monograph and will have open access to original dynamic visualizations, author interviews, and other interpretive content, along with social media tools to foster communities of scholars and history aficionados who share interests with the monograph's topics.

The first volume of this series, Sandra K. Sagala's *Buffalo Bill on the Silver Screen*, provides readers a detailed account of how William F. Cody worked with the emerging American film industry to promote America's frontier past and its legendary western characters, particularly himself. Cody's fascination with film reflected a long-held interest in using new technologies to bring his vision of the Wild West to the American public with ever-greater theatrical flair. Giving credit to Thomas Edison, Cody proclaimed that the phonograph provided the public "more entertainment and pleasure than any invention in the history of the world," and he would come to view Edison's film technology with similar appreciation. For William F. Cody, film was yet another invention to promote the Wild West—an invention that extended his ongoing use of railroads, mass-publishing, lithographic posters, electric lights, and sound recordings to publicize and enhance the performances of Buffalo Bill's Wild West. Sagala examines Cody's quest to authentically recreate his life experiences but also, driven by his business instincts, heighten the drama to stir his audiences. Cody hoped the revenue from his movies would cover past debts and secure his retirement from show business. Yet, as Sagala demonstrates, his hopes for quick financial gain eroded due to various legal claims to protect his name and image from competing film companies and vacillating audience demands.

From Joel McCrea's positive portrayal of the frontier hero to Paul Newman's negative depiction of the blowhard showman, "Hollywood" continued to present conflicting visions of William F.

Cody's life and legacy long after his death. Sandra K. Sagala's book reintroduces readers to the complex relationship between Cody and his public persona, "Buffalo Bill," as it played on, and behind, the silver screen.

Jeremy M. Johnston, Buffalo Bill Center of the West
Frank Christianson, Brigham Young University
Doug Seefeldt, Ball State University

Acknowledgments

While awaiting publication of my book *Buffalo Bill on Stage*, I revisited the Buffalo Bill Museum and Grave in Golden, Colorado. Director Steve Friesen asked what my next project would be. After some hemming and hawing on my part, he suggested I "do something" with Cody's movies. Here you go, Steve, with many thanks for your suggestions for improving the resultant manuscript.

It's a rare book that is solely the product of its author. Many people had unique roles in this one's development. First of all, to my family I owe much gratitude for their patience and encouragement. Acknowledgment and appreciation also go out to Phillip Blasco, Ray Phillips, Martin Grams Jr., David Kiehn, Allan Radbourne, Stan "Tex" Banash, David Phillips, Andrea Paling, Dawn and Sean McClung, Erika Castaño, Marilyn Nix, David Menefee, Marylin Schultz, and Tony Sapienza for sharing nuggets of information, photos, or letters.

A fellowship from the Cody Institute for Western American Studies allowed me to become immersed in Codyiana at the Buffalo Bill Historical Center in Cody, Wyoming, in Autumn

2008. For their part in making my western trip successful, I am grateful to Paul Fees, Robert Pickering, Kurt Graham, Mary Robinson, Megan Shaw Prelinger, Heidi Kennedy, Karling Abernathy, Lynn Houze, John Rumm, Diane Glass, Juti Winchester, and Leo Platteter. Thanks to Sheryl Long and Martha Allison-Otto of the Erie County Public Library's interlibrary loan department, who found some pretty elusive items. A promise to reciprocate goes to my beta readers, JoAnne Bagwell and Doreen Chaky. Finally, best wishes to editor Jay Dew at the University of Oklahoma Press for keeping the faith during the long approval process, to copy-editor John C. Thomas, and to project manager Alice K. Stanton.

Buffalo Bill
on the Silver Screen

Introduction

In December 1890, on a ridge above Dakota Territory's White Clay Creek, U.S. Army officers dismounted their horses to discuss the probability of war. In the enemy camp below, men searched the sky for signs of the coming storm, and a blanketed woman hurried into a tipi shadowed by campfires. In the morning, would these American Indians submit to white civilization or fight to the death to defend their culture and religion? When their messiah Wovoka preached the death of white men and the recovery of Indian lands, he had instigated a movement that frightened Indian agents and settlers and forced the army to intervene. As tribes danced to bring about the return of their dominance on the plains, army officials believed the time had come to deter any potential uprising. Both sides prepared for the conflict the dawn might bring.

Twenty-three years later, four now older men motored to the top of the same hill. Three generals and William Frederick Cody—Buffalo Bill, the Wild West showman—considered the activity below. The sights and sounds revived memories of those earlier days, but this night grease paint replaced war paint, blank cartridges replaced bullets, and instead of the boom of a Hotchkiss gun or a sorrowful Indian cry came the barking of a dog and children's playful shouts. The days "of worry and of warfare and of carnage" were over. The morrow's battle would only re-create the horrors both American Indians and Anglo-Americans suffered in the past, and no blood would spill. The tolling of the Angelus bell from the Catholic church now standing in place of the army's store returned the men's focus to the present. They climbed into their automobile and turned toward town. Cody eagerly awaited the dawn.[1]

For over thirty years William F. Cody proved his mastery at re-enacting events of the frontier. He entertained millions worldwide with demonstrations of cowboy and Indian life in his Wild West show. Over the course of his show business career, Cody thought of himself as an educator and recounted the horrific conflicts inherent in the settling of a nation. When the new technology of moving pictures exploded into the sphere of consumer entertainment, Cody, after first complaining about their usurping his Wild West business, embraced them, acting in and producing movies in which he did not fail to include the American Indian.[2]

No student of Buffalo Bill could deny that his life—whether as buffalo hunter, army scout, dramatic actor, or Wild West show-man—was engaged with Indians at every turn. He fought them, employed them, befriended them. Historians find his encounters with them detailed in army reports and in Wild West show programs. As uncomplicated as Cody's ambition, talent, and genius were, he was a man of complex contradictions when it came to his relationships with Indians. He defended their aggressive actions to a government intent on assimilation or annihilation, when staunch Indian fighters like generals William T. Sherman and Nelson A. Miles weren't sure whether or not "the only good

Indians are dead Indians." Three weeks after Custer's rout at Little Big Horn, Cody killed and scalped Yellow Hair (sometimes identified as Yellow Hand), a Cheyenne, at Nebraska's Warbonnet Creek, then replayed the slaying in his stage show and Wild West exhibition. Later he reenacted Custer's last stand with the words "Too Late" emblazoned on a backdrop, as if Cody's presence could have saved the general and his Seventh Cavalry. Sioux medicine man Sitting Bull had masterminded Custer's defeat, but Cody hired him to travel with his show, announcing they were "Foes in '76, Friends in '85." In newspaper interviews, Cody lamented the government's inability to deal with Indians after a hundred years' experience. So, despite their mutual respect, he would not negotiate treaties, mindful of the government's shameful record of breaking them.

He hired Indians at fair wages. If they became sick on tour, he paid their way home. When outsiders discriminated against them, Cody insisted on their being treated with equality. Once, when a hotel cook served them cold leftover pancakes for supper, Cody demanded they receive the same nourishing food as his white employees.[3] Despite his solicitude, critics brought charges of cruelty against him, leading to an official inquiry. The examiners concluded that his show Indians were "certainly the best looking and apparently the best fed Indians we have ever seen."[4]

Besides the invariable presence of Indians, America's frontier story too often involved wars over land, minerals, and ideals—wars for glory, ambition, and self-preservation. Wars had been a constant in Cody's life, and he reveled in the excitement and potential for personal glory. As a boy, he participated in Kansas/Missouri border skirmishes before his war record officially began with his enlistment in the Union Army in 1864. Five years later, as the Fifth Cavalry's chief scout, he alleged, contrary to the official report, that he killed Tall Bull, a renegade Cheyenne, in an engagement at Summit Springs, Colorado. At author Ned Buntline's urging, Cody turned to theatrical acting and fought red-painted actors in mock battles onstage. In the summer of 1876, again as chief scout, he led the "Dandy Fifth" to Warbonnet Creek and encountered Yellow Hair. Retiring his stage shows, he not only reenacted the Summit Springs and Warbonnet battles but fought off Indians as they pursued and threatened his Deadwood coach in the more expansive Wild West arena.

Buffalo Bill traveled throughout Europe during the 1890 season of the Ghost Dance but, upon his return to the States, he was asked by General Miles to attempt a peaceful arrest of Sitting Bull. Cody regretted his failure at the mission but was present for the Indians' surrender after the devastating Wounded Knee Creek debacle. By 1898 the United States was engaged in a war with Spain. Cody wrote a friend, "It's impossible for me to leave [my show] without some preparations and it will entail a big loss and my fortune naturally affect. But go I must. I have been in every war our country has back since bleeding Kansas war."[5] When the war's quick resolution precluded his attendance, he recorded a message supporting the president and modified Wild West acts to reflect the country's increasingly militaristic proclivities.

For the most part, wars were not foremost in the mind of the average American at the turn of the twentieth century. Instead, he would find it impossible to go about his daily business without being confronted by novel sights and sounds of a more peaceful nature. On his lunch break or before heading home, an assembly line laborer might stop at the neighborhood nickelodeon. He could spend weekends dancing to new music called jazz or attend professional baseball games. While politicians dealt with the pervasive problems of immigration, capitalism, and industrialism, the words and deeds of Cody's contemporaries like President Theodore Roosevelt, industrialist Henry Ford, and inventor Thomas Edison assured Americans the nation was evolving toward status as a major world power. Their philosophies and resourcefulness branded the entire era Progressive. Roosevelt believed progress was healthy but, for many, worries that the nation was moving too far too fast fueled nostalgia for the good old days.[6]

The Indians with whom Cody shared his Wild West livelihood enjoyed little of the ubiquitous progress. A few traveled with him around North America or Europe to see a world that otherwise would have remained a mystery, but the majority were shunted from one reservation of poor resources to another with even fewer life-sustaining necessities. Meanwhile, the many tribes, once feared by frontier settlers, surrendered their way of life to face another that many observers believed would lead to their extinction.

By 1913 the Wild West show through which Cody was acclaimed, censured, and eventually bankrupted garnered its final hurrahs. A few weeks after its sale at auction, he might have agreed with biographer John T. Morse, who wrote, "It's a queer condition; I find that I live only in the past, and yet am more than ever interested in the future,"[7] because at age sixty-seven Cody embarked on a final effort to generate wealth and reenact history. He gambled on moving pictures. In the panoply of America's new inventions, filmmaking caught Cody's fancy with its moneymaking possibilities and potential for preserving his legacy as frontier champion. Familiarity with moving pictures and experience as a performer enabled him to produce movies which, if attempted by anyone else, might be considered the apex of egoism. In the overall scheme of his entertainment career, it is regrettable that the films he made or those made about him appear inconsequential. Historians writing the narrative of early filmmakers and the development of the medium rarely report Cody's contributions. Nevertheless, his two films in particular—*The Life of Buffalo Bill* and *The Indian Wars*—document, more than any fictional retelling, events that actually took place not only in the life of one man but in America's western frontier.[8]

CHAPTER 1

The Advent of Western Movies

Every contrivance of man, every tool, every instrument, every utensil, every article designed for use, of each and every kind, evolved from a very simple beginning.

ROBERT COLLIER

Ironically, the horse, that icon of the West, provided the impetus for the development of moviemaking. In 1871, California railroad magnate Leland Stanford bet $25,000 on a popular debate over whether all of a horse's hooves left the ground during a gallop. To win the point, he teamed with British photographer Eadweard Muybridge. Five years and $50,000 in experiments later, Muybridge came up with a high-speed camera shutter. He spaced out a series of cameras connected to trip wires across a Sacramento racetrack. Both the horse and moving pictures were off and running. As it passed each camera, the horse tripped a wire, snapping a photograph. Lined up on a paper strip, the photographs proving that horses do briefly "fly" won Stanford his bet.[1]

Muybridge was not alone in discovering the mechanics of moving pictures. The idea also captivated Thomas Edison, who was generally credited with their invention, when in the late 1880s his resourceful assistant William K. L. Dickson incorporated a motion picture camera, which he called a kinetograph, and a viewing assembly, the kinetoscope. The latter, a boxlike structure housing a battery-powered mechanism, drove the film past a small incandescent lamp and a rapidly revolving shutter. The shutter exposed the flashing pictures to magnifying lenses through which a viewer looked. As one picture fell away another was exposed, creating moving pictures, much like a child's flip book.

During an 1889 trip to Paris for the Exposition Universelle, Edison met Cody, whose Wild West show was encamped outside Paris, when both celebrities attended the same soirée. As Edison reached the venue, Cody entered, "glittering in his well-known costume of white and gold, topped by his white ten-gallon hat, which he removed with a sweep that comprehended the whole audience."[2]

Cody invited Edison to an American-style breakfast at his camp, to which he had also asked other distinguished American tourists, including New York senator Chauncey M. Depew, U.S. minister Whitelaw Reid, and President Harrison's son.[3] Depew made a speech and Nate Salsbury, Cody's Wild West partner, shared amusing stories about life with a traveling show. Edison brought one of his phonographs, which "was put through its usual evolutions to the enjoyment of the whole audience."[4] During a camp tour, sharpshooter Annie Oakley cornered Edison to ask if he could design an electric gun. He told her he would consider it.[5]

At the afternoon's performance of the Wild West exhibition, five thousand spectators gave the inventor an ovation.[6] Carrying on his tradition, Cody invited Edison and Depew to ride the Deadwood coach "on its perilous journey" around the arena. A "savage horde of pesky redskins," some of the same Edison had encountered at the Eiffel Tower earlier in the week, chased the coach with mimic slaughter in mind. Later, at the Exposition, the American Indian performers listened to music and speeches on a phonograph cylinder. Edison's people then recorded Red Shirt shouting a war cry and played it back for the others' astonishment.[7]

It may have been at this demonstration that Cody praised Edison's invention: "It is a great pleasure to see this wonder working man at his task. . . . It seems almost uncanny that the voice in this place can be perpetuated and that he has set out to the world his phonograph, which have given more entertainment and pleasure than any invention in the history of the world."[8]

While he was in Paris, Edison also visited Étienne-Jules Marey, whose experiments with moving pictures involved paper-based film. Edison returned to his New Jersey laboratory to refine the kinetoscope so the viewer peeking through a slit in the top of the machine could watch a minute-long moving picture on a paper strip. Two years later, when Mrs. Edison hosted a meeting of the Federation of Women's Clubs, her husband allowed the ladies to view a film through his new peephole contraption. By August 1893 the "Wizard of Menlo Park," having worked industriously on "an instrument which does for the Eye what the phonograph does for the Ear," received a patent for a motion picture camera.[9]

Cody and Edison met again when Chicago hosted the 1893 World's Columbian Exposition, where both men expected to "make a big splash." Before it opened, Edison's partners received permission to exhibit 150 motion picture viewers to solicit national and worldwide orders. The problem was, though the prototype was ready, Edison did not have many machines or films for them. Eager to exhibit them, he had nevertheless done little to guarantee their appearance. When weather delayed the Exposition's opening, it seemed possible the kinetoscopes might be ready, but the Panic of 1893 jeopardized Edison's other interests and took his time and energy away from the picture machine. None appeared at the Exposition, and another year would pass before they were ready for sale. Still, Edison enjoyed talking about his "happy combination of photography and electricity."[10]

Despite his rejection for a spot at the Exposition on grounds of "incongruity," Cody opened his Wild West show on nearby acreage and attracted over twenty-seven million visitors. Fair managers would rue the day they judged Cody's show "not refined enough" to be an official exhibit.[11] Besides his stock reenactments of the Pony Express, Buffalo Hunt, and Custer's Charge, Russian, German, French, British, and American soldiers competed in military maneuvers while Syrians, Arabians, and Mexicans demonstrated horsemanship. With such all-encompassing representations, no wonder spectators believed they had seen the entire World's Fair in one performance. One of the worst recessions in America's economic history notwithstanding, Cody did a resounding business, netting nearly a million dollars.

While Cody was entertaining with displays of shooting, riding, and a reality of a West he considered still relevant, a comparatively unknown historian was making news at the American Historical Association in downtown Chicago. Frederick Jackson Turner read his thesis on the frontier's significance in American history, explaining how its settlement formed distinctly American characteristics and influenced the country's future. While Turner focused on "the closing of a great historic movement," Cody's program recounted the "rapidly extending frontier." The historian and the showman described American Indians first as obstacles to western settlement, then as woeful reminders of a bygone era. In show acts, Indians, fulfilling every dime-novel reader's expectations, portrayed stereotyped warlike savages and play-acted attacks on innocent settlers and ill-fated soldiers. In light of Cody's honoring his "ambition . . . to instruct and educate the Eastern public to respect the denizens of the West by giving them a true, untinselled representation of a page of frontier history that is fast passing away," journalist Brick Pomeroy endorsed the exhibition's reality and wished for "more progressive educators like William Cody in this world."[12]

His show performed frequently in New Jersey where, in West Orange, workers had built the world's first motion picture studio. William Dickson referred to it as "The Kinetographic Theater;"

Edison called it a "dog house," but it was more familiarly known as "Black Maria" for its resemblance to a patrol wagon. Black tarpaper covered the 15- by 50-foot exterior; steel wheels underneath each end allowed it to pivot on a circular wooden track. Its sharply pitched roof opened to allow sunlight to stream onto the interior stage.[13]

With the large cumbersome kinetograph camera, Dickson began taking scenes on short strips of film. Initially he could record only one or two performances, then needed a week to process fifteen seconds of usable footage. Edison's camera operators used ordinary events as the first cinematic subjects: a man sneezing, a prize fight, two boxing cats. Once journalists publicized the need, dancers, acrobats, and vaudeville acts of all kinds offered to perform before the camera for no remuneration except a "sumptuous dinner." Edison himself thought the motion picture idea, though fine for fun, would not be profitable and estimated that about ten kinetoscopes would suffice for the entire country.[14]

He was wrong. A year after the Columbian Exposition, the first kinetoscope parlor opened in New York City. For the first time, commercial movies were available to patrons, who paid to look at a different film on each of ten machines. In the beginning, kinetoscopes were quite profitable, but the novelty wore off for want of new films and because only one customer could use a machine at a time.[15]

Profits picked up when inventors devised projectors that enabled several people to view a film simultaneously. Enterprising exhibitors set up "theaters" in narrow storefronts with as many chairs as would fit and charged ten cents admittance. "It was too much," protested the press. When they lowered the price to five cents, such theaters became known as "nickelodeons." The idea caught on like "a frenzy," so that by 1905 theaters were "multiplying faster than guinea pigs" and attracting nearly two million viewers daily from early morning until midnight. Exhibitors

enticed customers with megaphone calls or shocking promotional posters. Because early films were frequently "blood-and-
thunder types" and included murders or train robberies, they
held little didactic value. Nevertheless, *Moving Picture World*, a
film industry journal, recognized that "the possibilities of them
in an education way are unlimited."[16]

Contemporary critics arrived at similar conclusions about
the phenomenon. In March 1912, Henry Spurr observed that
the cinematograph (the projector) had "created nearly fifteen
million new [motion picture] theater goers in the last ten years."
Harold Edwards wondered if anyone would ever again pay two
dollars to see actors onstage when they could see them more
cheaply in pictures.[17] "Everyone," wrote W. Stephen Bush, a
Moving Picture World columnist, "young and old, rich and poor,
intelligent and ignorant," was going to the movies.[18] Cinema's
appeal soon led to a need for longer and more complex films,
forcing filmmakers to develop narratives with decent plots and
thorough characterizations. "The people want a story," one
manager said. "More story, larger story, better story, with plenty
of action"—requisites even now characterizing popular films.[19]

In 1903, Edison cameraman Edwin S. Porter became one of
the first to produce, direct, and edit a narrative film set in the
West—*The Great Train Robbery*. Railroad holdups still made headlines; two years previously, Butch Cassidy and his Wild Bunch
failed in their attempt to rob the Great Northern. Porter's twelve-
minute film combined essential elements of a now-familiar western:
villains performing a dastardly deed, good guys in pursuit, a long
chase, and comeuppance for the outlaws. The unique film from
the wilds of New Jersey's Essex County Park along the Lackawanna
Railroad scarcely looked authentically western, but the subject
launched a renewed fervor for the genre.

Classic melodramatic archetypes from literature and theater—
the handsome hero, villainous blackguard, savage Indian, and
beautiful maiden—were readily adapted to western film plots.

The scenery was already supplied by nature; inherent violence prevailed in the story line. One historian concluded, "All the actor had to do was don the proper costume, mount the proper horse, and he was ready to head for the nearest hills."[20] As American history presented filmmakers with an inexhaustible supply of subjects, true frontiersmen like Kit Carson, Daniel Boone, and Bill Cody presaged the filmic hero. Because a western's impact was not dependent on its faithfulness to history, filmmakers could revise events or reinvent historical characters. They found that westerns, being "distinctly American in characterization, scenery and surroundings," replete with men who portrayed the American ideal of resolute integrity, were the kind of wholesome, educational entertainment *Moving Picture World* suggested they offer.[21]

One of the extras in *The Great Train Robbery* was Max Aronson, who would change his name and gain fame as Gilbert "Broncho Billy" Anderson. After working as director, scriptwriter, cameraman, and actor for various film companies, he and George K. Spoor merged their talents and initials to form the Essanay (S 'n' A) Film Manufacturing Company. Essanay headquartered on Argyle Street in Chicago, but Anderson appreciated audiences' growing sophistication and demand for authentic backgrounds. After the *New York Dramatic Mirror* derided nonwestern westerns as amateurish and insisted that "cowboys, Indians and Mexicans must be seen in proper scenic backgrounds to convey any impression of reality," Anderson regularly traveled to Colorado and New Mexico seeking not only year-round favorable weather but broad western vistas as well. He and Spoor opened a California branch of the company in Niles while maintaining the Chicago center with its three studios, carpentry and props departments, and film-processing laboratories.[22]

During Wild West shows' off-season, filmmakers hired unemployed show people to act as extras, and working cowboys lined up to serve as consultants or actors. The performers brought along their costumes and props, but filmmakers also borrowed equipment and copied stunts and narratives. Routinely filming outdoors to take advantage of the scenery, Essanay could honestly advertise its westerns as genuine, "made in the West . . . amidst scenes of beauty."[23] The preponderance of early films are lost, but one estimate holds that by 1910 westerns comprised about 20 percent of films released in the United States. Several filmmakers chose to specialize in the genre and planned to release two reels every week, an achievement surpassed by Anderson, who once made seven one-reel films in a week.[24]

Although most uninformed eastern audiences accepted westerners' cinematic adventures as realistic, one *Moving Picture News* editor denounced the films "as far from being true to life as it is possible for anything to be." Indulging in the sensational, producers created characters "never known in everyday life." Protagonists operated within improbable scenes and often degenerated from wholesome heroes to desperadoes. Eventually audiences, so "satiated with this sort of food that they are turning in disgust against it," began to "grumble in a pretty loud manner."[25] Stephen Bush chastised exhibitors for showing graphic westerns that attracted "crowds of rowdies" and allowed "scorbutic-looking youths with atrophied brain cells" to frighten "desirable people" away. Aggravated complainers objected to a "screen full of the smother of Western desperadoes' guns, dynamite explosions, or torrents of gore."[26]

Rival critics argued that the sensationalism depicted authenticity. One wistfully contrasted the civilization and order of city life with the "savage forces of Nature" that "primeval man, with all his passions" had to confront.[27] Nevertheless, the public spoke with their dollars, so by 1913 western filmmakers had toned down their heroes' lurid adventures, making them more palatable and "deferential to traditional values."[28]

If producers expected their westerns to be at all credible, besides reducing the hyperbole they had to include American Indians.

Again, numbers vary, but most historians agree that at least one hundred films featuring Indians were released between 1910 and 1913.[29] In most stories involving conflicts between Indians and whites, the tribes revealed a moral superiority, having a greater sense of honor, mercy, and altruism. *Moving Picture World* applauded such characterizations depicting the Indians' "noble traits."[30]

Like their cowboy counterparts, American Indians often worked, and played their roles well, in the western movies. But however genuine they might look at times, some were only whites "sufficiently well made up to pass as such."[31] Directors found themselves defending the employment of whites in Indian roles: "We tried our best to make [the Indians] act, but they wouldn't do it. . . . The Indians . . . found it impossible to move about and behave in the manner of stage Indians and their work was pronounced impossible."[32] To aggravate matters, filmmakers, careless with details, regularly mixed up tribes, putting Sioux bonnets on southwestern tribes or showing Manhattan Islanders dwelling in skin tipis used only by tribes beyond the Mississippi.[33] Indian critics especially condemned the lack of authenticity. John Standing Horse at the Carlisle Indian School ridiculed directors for simply sticking chicken feathers in the women's hair. "It is funny, but they would all look much better without them. . . . Have also seen pictures with all the made-up Indian men with big war bonnets on their heads. Another big laugh."[34]

The real challenge for western filmmakers, wrote historian Jon Tuska, had been "to interpret [the West's] spirit and give it a new meaning."[35] Though Cody sympathized with and supported Indian rights, his Wild West spectacles depicting "A Prairie Emigrant Train Crossing the Plains" and "The Capture of the Deadwood Mail Coach by the Indians" demonstrated unequivocal white conquest. He deflected criticisms of racism or exploitation by befriending Sitting Bull and the other show Indians. American Indian author Vine Deloria, Jr., commended Cody for employing individuals whom the Bureau of Indian

Affairs considered dangerous when touring with him saved them from imprisonment. Deloria also approved of Cody's including them in his "Congress of Rough Riders." "Instead of degrading the Indians and classifying them as primitive savages," Deloria wrote, "Cody elevated them to a status of equality with contingents from other nations" by recognizing their skills as warriors.[36]

After the final Indian war in 1890, it may have seemed that the remaining tribes were on their way to successful integration. Fearsome leaders, including Crazy Horse and Sitting Bull, were dead. Tribal governments aligned with U.S. laws, and Indian-owned farms proliferated. Some Indians gained citizenship and had their children educated in Christian schools. No longer threatening, they were assimilating into "just plain Americans."[37]

Various exhibitions had featured Indians since the mid-eighteenth century, but eastern audiences had not seen enough of them close at hand to question the realism of their on-screen portrayal. Because a fictional Indian story was shown on the same movie screen as factual newsreels, audiences trusted the filmic depiction as also being accurate. Producers catered to filmgoers with anti-Indian prejudices by portraying Indians as savage villains. When the popularity of those plots waned, depictions of Indians as sympathetic and honorable characters gained favor. Almost invariably, however, they became "good" only when they abandoned tradition in favor of white civilization.[38]

Buffalo Bill would eventually take the truth of Anglo/Indian interactions to an extreme, showing audiences a realism previously unconsidered.

CHAPTER 2

The First Studio Filming

I never did a day's work in my life. It was all fun.
THOMAS A. EDISON

William Cody and Thomas Edison exemplified the characteristics Frederick Jackson Turner credited to frontiersmen: "that practical, inventive turn of mind, quick to find expedients; that masterful grasp of material things, lacking in the artistic but powerful to effect great ends." Edison, who claimed, "Show me a thoroughly satisfied man and I will show you a failure," found in Cody a kindred spirit. Cody's endeavors to educate the eastern masses about life in the West also appealed to Edison, who believed he could teach more history in fifteen minutes with a motion picture than could be learned from any book. The showman's narrative style and the inventor's machines complemented each other as well, and the men would be among the first using the medium of movies to tell the nation's history.[1]

In the summer of 1894, Cody's months-long contract had him exhibiting his Wild West at Ambrose Park in Brooklyn. Near season's end, the Edison Electric Illuminating Company invited over two hundred members of the New York Electrical Society to inspect the park's lighting plant. It included two searchlight beams

18

capable of precisely following the flying glass ball targets of sharp-shooters Cody, Johnny Baker, and Annie Oakley. The electricians stayed to watch the performance.[2]

Since the kinetograph's invention, Edison had wanted to ascertain if it was sensitive enough to follow the flight of a bullet.[3] He may have invited Cody to come to his studio and shoot before the camera, or it may have been Cody's idea as publicity for his upcoming European tour. Because of their popularity as entertainers, Edison was also pleased to film the show's Indians. On Monday, September 24, 1894, Cody, along with several members of the Brulé and Ogallala tribes—chiefs Last Horse, Parts His Hair, and Black Cat; young men Hair Coat, Charging Crow, Dull Knife, Holy Bear, Crazy Bear, Strong Talker, Pine, Little Eagle, Young Bear, and Runs About; and boys Johnny No Neck Burke and Seven Up—took the train to West Orange, New Jersey. Accompanying them were interpreter John Changrau, Cody's publicist John Burke, scout Jack Stillwell, and advertising agent F. Madden.[4]

Cody started the demonstration with some rapid shooting. Edison himself spent little time behind the camera, so William Dickson acted as producer; his associate William Heise manned the camera. The Kinetoscope Company's May 1895 catalog described the completed film as "a fine picture of the principal, and beautiful smoke effects" and priced it at $12.50. Upon viewing it, a Melbourne, Australia, newspaperman wrote, "Buffalo Bill moves a living personality before you, and will move a hundred years hence when he has grown up into daisies and grass."[5]

When Edison historian Ray Phillips found photographs in Dickson's 1895 book *History of the Kinetograph, Kinetsocope and Kinetophonograph* showing sixteen frames of the action, he and several colleagues re-created the film by copying the frames onto modern film. They show Cody on one knee, aiming and shooting his repeating rifle, then moving the rifle lever down as smoke billows from the barrel. To complete the sequence as Edison's camera originally captured it, Phillips needed to reverse the last seven frames so Cody seemed to work the lever in order to shoot again. Reversing the frames, however, caused the smoke to appear to blow back into the barrel. Dean Sadamune, director of computer graphics at International Creative Effects, used a photoediting computer program to effectively erase the cloud of smoke. After further enhancements, the result was twenty-three frames of film which, when run repeatedly, show Cody shooting as he did in 1894.[6]

Then the Indians stepped onto Black Maria's stage. As light filtered through the roof, the eldest, Chief Last Horse, brandished his tomahawk. The "howling, painted savages" were dressed in breechcloths, moccasins, and body paint. Several wore bone breastplates; two bore large headdresses or had embellished their hair with feathers. They stood and faced front as if waiting for a signal. Heise prepared the camera, and Dickson called out that he too was ready.

At John Changrau's cry "Kai-ya!" the men began to dance clockwise in a circle. Somehow aware this was a rare opportunity, the younger men, like Hair Coat, resorted to shoving Last Horse from the foreground and appear to fight for center stage as the two children squirm around. The constraints of performing in a space about twelve feet square hindered their ability to perform the dance on its usual scale, so they appear unnaturally crushed together. The two-minute film is dark and the action not very clear, possibly because of the age of the extant film or an overcast sky on the day of filming. In some copies, in the lower right corner, a handwritten sign reads BUFFALO BILL'S WILD WEST S, with the rest of the word SHOW missing.[7] Without evidence that the movements were indeed that of the Ghost Dance, the film was so named when, the next day, the New York Herald commented on the "memorable engagement" and reminded its readers that the 1890 battle of Wounded Knee was no doubt still fresh in the warriors' minds.

Besides marking the beginning of cinematic commercialization of Indians, the filming was "probably more effective in demonstrating to the red men the power and supremacy of the white man, for savagery and the most advanced science stood face to face." A contemporary price guide described it as "one of the most peculiar customs of the Sioux" and charged distributors $7.50. A copy of the film is available for viewing at the George Eastman House in Rochester, New York; the Library of Congress; the Academy of Motion Picture Arts and Sciences in Los Angeles; and the Archives du film du Centre National de la Cinématographie, Bois d'Arcy, France.[8]

The next event was a war council in which Cody and Last Horse converse in sign language. Last Horse "guyed" Cody, the interpreter said, and all the Indians had a good laugh. They passed the "wampum belt" and smoked a peace pipe. Most likely it was Dickson who then photographed the entire party.[9]

The session concluded with the filming of a Buffalo Dance. The handwritten logo "MB" (for Maguire and Baucus) appears on some copies at the top left of each frame.[10] Franck Maguire, an agent for Edison Phonograph, and Joseph Baucus, of a Wall Street legal firm, became Edison's official agents for marketing the kinetoscope in Europe and negotiated sales of films made in the Black Maria for exclusive use in kinetoscopes. Several copies survive at New York's Museum of Modern Art; the French archives at Bois d'Arcy; and the Library of Congress. Throughout, Strong Talker and Pine sit cross-legged and beat drums as Last Horse, Parts His Hair, and Hair Coat dance in a circle. Sound recording was not available, but they sing as though they were on the plains and, with threatening looks toward the camera, wave their weapons because "they had been told the strange thing pointed at them would show them to the world until after the sun had slept his last sleep."[11]

Each of the black-and-white films ran 50 feet, the exact length early projectors could hold. Throughout the hour-long filming, Edison's wife and daughter looked on at the strange attraction. Reporting the event, the *New York Press* hoped that "long after the red man has left his last trace, perhaps a perfect representation of his dances will be before the coming generation, perpetuated by Wizard Edison's unique and wonderful invention."[12] Returning to New York, Last Horse, his face still smeared with yellow paint, flirted with a woman who sat opposite him on the train. When he "glanced meaningful at her and breathed hard," she stalked off, muttering about him being a "dreadful beast."[13]

After the Wild West show closed on October 6, most of the troupe boarded a ship to Europe. However, several performers headed back to West Orange to be filmed. Pedro Esquivel and Dionecio Gonzales performed a Mexican knife duel. Vincente Oropeza threw a lasso and, from the show's Far East portion, came sheiks Hadj Tahar and Hadj L. Cheriff. Nine days after Cody's departure, cowboy star Lee Martin and Frank Hammitt, Wild West cowboy and equestrian manager, arrived with "an unusually wicked broncho." Because of the Black Maria's small interior, Dickson fenced in an area behind the studio. When Martin mounted the horse Sunfish, Hammitt sat on the fence and fired his six-shooter to enliven the action. The Wild West's top sharpshooter, Annie Oakley, debuted on film November 1, in a short fringed skirt and jacket. She fired at balloons mounted on a board, changed rifles, then shot at glass balls her husband Frank Butler, in derby hat and vest, tossed up.[14]

Edison and other early moviemakers continued to improve the motion picture camera and projector and, because of the show's popularity, "practiced" on Cody's Wild West several times. The Library of Congress holds an 1896 or 1897 film by France's Lumière brothers containing scenes of costumed Indians dancing and riding horseback, titled *La Cirque Buffalo Bill: Peaux Rouges* (The Circus of Buffalo Bill: Redskins).[15] James White of the kineto-scope company assumed the role of producer and worked with cameraman William Heise. On May 8, 1897, Heise filmed Cody at Grant's tomb in New York. Listed as *Buffalo Bill and Escort*, the 50-foot film shows Cody on a chestnut stallion leading a company of cavalry. When Heise filmed Wild West parades on May 20, 1898, in Newark, New Jersey, using a newer, mobile camera, the seventeen minutes documented two segments of the spectacle including covered wagons, cavalrymen, and Indians in full-feathered bonnets. Crowds watch as eight horses draw a gilt coach; Cody and his Rough Riders follow. The second sequence presents the same parade with the entire procession of mounted cavalry, Indians, Arabs, Cossacks, and a host of other riders.[16] Four weeks later, the film was ready for viewing and is now housed at the Library of Congress.

When William Dickson left Edison's employ, he and three others formed American Mutoscope and Biograph, which soon became Edison's chief competitor. In April 1900, while the Wild West again exhibited at Ambrose Park, cameraman Frederick S. Armitage filmed 566 feet of the show. Armitage returned a month later with cameraman Arthur Marvin to film the Wild West parade three times to double the previous footage. A year later he filmed the parade down New York City's Fifth Avenue. The Biograph Company set up another camera in the arena to capture galloping cowboys and Indians moving diagonally past as Cody introduced the Rough Riders to the spectators.

When Sigmund Lubin formed a film company as an offshoot of his manufacturing business, one of his first projects was also the filming of Wild West show segments.[17] Viewers can see them on the Library of Congress American Memory website.[18] A date of July 2, 1902, is listed under the title of the film, suggesting a release date and not the date of filming, since nearly everyone in the scenes wears a winter overcoat. Parade participants include cowboys, Indians, and U.S. Cavalry soldiers on horseback. From the saddle of his white steed, Cody doffs his hat to the crowd. The Selig Polyscope Company of Chicago, founded by former vaudevillian-turned-photographer William Selig, shot 200 feet of similar footage.

Meanwhile, back in the West in 1902, workmen completed construction of Buffalo Bill's Irma Hotel in the town of Cody,

"Try some of these waters," Cody might be saying to his friends at Demaris Springs. (Buffalo Bill Historical Center, Cody, Wyo., video no. 25)

Wyoming. Situated fifty miles from the entrance to Yellowstone Park, Cody had first planned the town's location farther west, nearer Demaris Springs. Because the sulphurous water was reputed to have therapeutic powers, he planned to bottle it and sell it at the Wild West's concession, ultimately hoping to entice visitors to the area. A cameraman was on hand when Cody accompanied friends to the springs. On the film, he sips from a cup and invites the others to do the same with a "Here, try some," gesture.

In 1962, Cody's biographer Don Russell gave a presentation for the Chicago Westerners about Cody's films. Member Archer Jackson had found a 300-foot, two-reel film available in 8 and 16 mm at Blackhawk Films of Davenport, Iowa, a business dedicated to collecting and preserving classic moving pictures.[19]

In the first reel—*Buffalo Bill's Wild West 1898–1910*—Cody is at his tent on show grounds. He mounts his horse, possibly Duke, which he acquired in 1898. A grand entry opens the show with the Indians parading by tribe: Cheyennes, Ogallalas, Arapahos, and Brulés. The Rough Riders carry flags identifying them variously as Mexican vaqueros, British cavalry, Russian Cossacks, Arabs, Japanese cavalry, or U.S. cavalry. Cody rides to the front, sweeps off his hat and, with a bow, announces, "Ladies and Gentlemen, may I present to you a Congress of Rough Riders of the World."

The second reel shows a six-mule team pulling the Deadwood stagecoach, an original property since the show's inception in 1883. Several films capture the cavalry repelling an Indian attack on the coach, one of the show's most popular acts. Unfortunately, none shows any of its famous passengers such as the kings of Denmark, Greece, Belgium, and Saxony, who rode in it during the 1887 exhibition in London.[20] On that occasion, Cody reportedly quipped to the Prince of Wales, "I have held four kings [in poker] more than once . . . but, your Highness, I never held four kings and the royal joker before."[21]

CHAPTER 3

Filming the Wild West

I have seen your Wild West show. . . . Down to its smallest
details, the show is genuine.

MARK TWAIN TO WILLIAM CODY, 1884

During the Wild West's week-long stay in Philadelphia in June
1907, moviemakers filmed various acts, some footage of which
remains. The Summit Springs battle reenactment opened with
Indians representing Chief Tall Bull's Dog Soldiers on the
march with travois, horses, and dogs. They set up a camp of tipis,
stretching skins over lodge poles while horses wander aimlessly
in front of the camera. Indian women manhandle two white
women as a few men dance and others sit cross-legged smoking
pipes. When a lookout spots approaching cavalry, the Indians
wrestle their captives into the tipi. Cowboys dressed as soldiers
arrive to the rescue. In the ensuing battle, "wounded" Indians
roll around on the ground, still swinging their lances. One white
woman is "killed," and a trooper helps the other onto his horse.[1]

In the segment "Buffalo Hunt," Cody demonstrates how he
chased and shot buffalo on the plains. Don Russell considered
it one of the show's most difficult sequences because the animals
were unpredictable and, unlike horses, impossible to train.[2] Cody

exhibits his marksmanship in the next sequence, shooting at glass balls a cowboy riding alongside him tosses into the air.

Beginning a "Life on the Ranch" segment, Cody scoops water from a trough with his hat. After man and horse drink their fill, Cody pats water on his head and on the horse's forelock. With no segue into the next action, cowboys and cowgirls dance a quadrille on horseback—one of many captured on film—but the fun ends when Indians attack. Three cowboys simulate being shot by forcing their horses to the ground.

Johnny Baker was a sort of adopted son who, as a youngster, met Cody in North Platte and tagged along when he started the Wild West show. Billed as "the Cowboy Kid," Baker excelled in various marksmanship stunts including shooting while standing on his head or leaning backwards over a stool. After footage of such a performance, a spectacle titled "Cowboy Fun" showcases talented riders scooping objects from the ground while on horseback and lassoing wild horses. Then vaquero Vincente Oropeza, champion of the lasso, demonstrates his twirling.

One spectacle is missing from extant scenes. After Porter's *The Great Train Robbery* had been a decided hit with movie audiences, circus showmen—Cody included—were on the lookout for a comparable attraction. Arthur Voegtlin, copyright holder of the dramatic spectacle of the same title, had, after "vigorous bidding," awarded exclusive rights to Gordon W. "Pawnee Bill" Lillie to produce in his western show. Equipment for the presentation included a 30-ton engine, passenger coaches, portable mountains, railroad tracks, dance halls, gambling houses, even a 100,000-gallon reservoir. Voegtlin promised injunctions against other showmen who ignored his copyright.[3]

As a young boy, Pawnee Bill had watched with wide eyes and mouth agape at Cody's histrionics in the melodrama *Scouts of the Plains* in Lillie's hometown of Bloomington, Illinois. Inspired by the dramatics, Lillie went west and secured a secretary's position at

Oklahoma's Pawnee agency. Gaining knowledge of the Pawnee culture and a grasp of the language, Lillie became an interpreter with Cody's Wild West, eventually branching out with his own Historical Wild West, Mexican Hippodrome, Indian Museum and Grand Fireworks Exhibition and giving his mentor Cody some real competition. By 1900, in his search for a unique angle, Lillie had added a Great Far East contingent, including Hindu snake charmers and South Sea Islanders.

Ignoring threats of lawsuit, Cody adopted "The Great Train Hold-up and the Bandit Hunters of the Union Pacific." Program notes boasted that his company included several men who had participated in train robberies "notable for their daring and for the consequences which attended them." His prop men reproduced a portable locomotive and railroad cars. During the performance, the robbers signal the train to stop, enter the express car and remove the safe, but, unable to open it, they resort to dynamite. The explosion alerts lawmen, who pursue the outlaws to the mountains. After a shootout, when the dead and wounded are put on board and passengers have returned to their seats, the train departs.[4]

Only a few months into Cody's production, Voegtlin made good on his promise to seek an injunction against those presenting his property without paying royalties. Cody's lawyer claimed he had a right to use the title and the effects after obtaining them from William T. Keogh, a dramatic manager with a play running under that name. Voegtlin's attorney, Judge Dittenhoefer, specified that his client claimed exclusive rights not to the use of a railway engine but to the idea of having a female robber flag the train. In his rebuttal, Cody's lawyer contended that the showman had been thinking of staging a holdup for twenty years, causing Dittenhoefer to wonder if Cody also had the female robber "in his mind or elsewhere 20 years ago." U.S. Circuit Court Judge Lacombe made no decision, and Cody proceeded to feature the attraction for several years.[5]

Shortly after the 1907 Wild West season began, financial panic again gripped the country. When families lacked extra money for entertainment, all areas of amusement felt the strain. To pay previous years' expenses, Cody had borrowed money from his Wild West partner, former circus man James Bailey. When Bailey died in 1906, his estate held half interest in Cody's show as well as a $12,000 note from Cody, who had no proof that he had repaid it. Between the Bailey family's demands and the poor economy, Cody constantly worried about money. The show that was to finance his investments in mining and real estate was barely making enough to support itself. He needed a new partner to manage the show's capital while he continued to perform. That someone had to not only help sustain the show through the summers but support the expense of its winter quarters.[6]

When Pawnee Bill Lillie offered to buy out Bailey's interest, Cody was at first reluctant to discuss a merger. He was, however, impressed with Lillie's business acumen. The two Bills finally agreed to combine their shows for the 1909 season into Buffalo Bill's Wild West and Pawnee Bill's Far East, a deal effectively rescuing Cody from bankruptcy. Attendance and profits increased under Lillie's management. Lillie reaped the benefits, too, but was more financially solvent than Cody. Having paid $50,000 for a third interest, midway through the season he paid $66,000 more and acquired sole ownership of the show.[7]

Over the years, essays in the Wild West program guide tutored audiences on American Indian culture. One, titled "The Indian's Education," explained that Cody taught "almost as many Indians as have the Government schools," showing them "the power and magnitude of the white race." Cody hoped the "enlightened individual" would share with his tribe the "wonders which have been unfolded before his bewildered, but believing, eyes." Having seen countless white men, Indians would forget "any silly notions" involving war. Cody reminded his audience that the Indians were "among the survivors of a fast-disappearing race; the true, and genuinely original American" but alas, "doomed . . . to extinction like the buffalo they once hunted." As a result of years of forced movement from their homes, lack of substantial and nourishing annuities, and a government policy condoning annihilation, the 1890 census counted fewer than 300,000 American Indians.[8] It seemed they were indeed on their way to extinction.

Rodman Wanamaker shared the foregone conclusion. When he inherited his father's department store (later Macy's), he hired former minister Joseph K. Dixon to lecture in the store's educational department. Dixon, in his enthusiasm for Indian welfare and conviction that the tribes would soon vanish from the land, convinced Wanamaker to finance three expeditions "to perpetuate the life story of these first Americans" and their customs, sports, warfare, and religion. Dixon's 1908 and 1909 tours of reservations resulted in hundreds of photographs, a cinematic version of *The Song of Hiawatha,* and a book titled *The Vanishing Race.*[9]

Commending Cody for his "honorable work among the Indians," for having stood "eternally for justice to the Red Man," and for having "paved the way in this gigantic work . . . [of] reproducing in permanent form the story of Indian Life and character," Wanamaker and Dixon welcomed him to the department store on May 12, 1909. Wanamaker presented his guest a leather-bound portfolio containing pages of elaborate calligraphic text extolling the showman's accomplishments. He also used the occasion and accompanying publicity to announce his plan to build a statue of the American Indian in New York Harbor. Rivaling Lady Liberty in size, its purpose was for all to understand "the welcome given in years gone to the early settlers by the red man."[10]

Back at the Wild West showground, a new worry emerged. Since 1893, George W. Miller and his three sons had worked a ranch on 110,000 Oklahoma acres. In 1907 they decided to branch out into show business, calling themselves the Miller

Brothers 101 show. Unlike Cody's emphasis on Indians and frontier settlement, the Millers took ranching as inspiration and featured cowboys' trick riding and fancy roping. Their national and international success brought the outfit to the attention of western filmmakers.[11]

Not only were the Millers usurping Cody's arena business, they offered their ranch as a site for location films. Whereas Cody paid to idle his Wild West show over the winter, the Millers were hired by the New York Motion Picture Company under the Bison brand, which set them up in California. With director Thomas Ince in charge, their company worked year-round and clinched Ince's reputation as a pioneer in western filmmaking.[12] Such early efforts focused primarily on documenting western arena shows, but filmmakers began to realize that moving pictures could also candidly chronicle the story of the West.

Despite behind-the-scenes financial scrambling and increasing ill health of its star, Cody's Wild West continued to impress audiences. The *Illinois State Journal* credited the "genuineness of the entertainers and the originality of their efforts" in creating the "diversified entertainment." Notwithstanding the best talents of the cowboys and Indians, "the real original" Buffalo Bill's name and achievements drew in the crowds. Little more than a figurehead since partnering with Lillie, even at that "Cody himself [was] more interesting than his famed show."[13]

But, at sixty-four years of age, retirement was on his mind. He told Lillie, "You know . . . by the time our season closes I am just about all in. The constant noise and turmoil both days and nights just wears on a fellows nerves." According to Lillie's memoirs, Cody asked him how he'd like to make a million dollars. Lillie was all for it as long as he didn't have to kill anyone or rob a bank. Cody explained his impression that, if people thought they had only one more chance to ever see him again, they would flock to the show. In two seasons they could cover America and Canada and "make a million dollars each season." Cody added,

"I do not expect to live more than a couple of hundred years, and if I am ever to get any rest, pleasure, and recreation, I must do it pretty soon."[14]

At the opening of the 1910 season, seven thousand fans packed Madison Square Garden. When the grand showman rode into the arena, he waited five minutes for the cheering to subside before speaking his sorrowful good-byes. Cody told of his gratitude for the appreciation easterners had shown him; he talked about the American Indian, whose virtual disappearance made way for homesteaders. He hoped to return to New York, he said, "but not as a showman in the saddle." Then he waved his hat and slowly backed his horse toward the exit.[15]

After years of watching Cody's name, experience, and show-manship make him money on a grand scale and learning of the plan to close the show, Pliny P. Craft, agent for the Patrick A. Powers Motion Picture Company, approached Pawnee Bill on the show lot at Williamsport, Pennsylvania, on May 26, 1910, with $1,000 in hand. Powers, who would eventually join Carl Laemmle at Universal Film Manufacturing Company, and Craft predicted a profitable venture in filming a biography of the showmen and explained their idea to "take, make and sell or exhibit films of Western Frontier life and episodes real or imagined." The two Bills didn't even have to appear in the film; their names alone would enhance its value. If they did, "it would be even better"; otherwise look-alike stand-ins could take their parts. After proffering the $1,000, Craft promised $25,000 more with an additional $5,000 deposited in a Mt. Vernon bank to guarantee payments.[16]

The men hammered out a contract on June 4 that put Craft and Powers in business as the Buffalo Bill and Pawnee Bill Film Company. *Moving Picture World* announced Cody and Lillie's move into the fledgling industry. One film would illustrate events in which the showmen had participated and include the Wild West show's entire roster. A second two-reel film would chronicle Cody's life from boyhood to the present.[17]

To direct, Craft hired German-born Paul Panzer, who would later star with Pearl White in *The Perils of Pauline*. Harry Davis and John P. Harris, theater managers famous for having coined the phrase "nickelodeon" and already in business with Craft, would produce.[18] Two weeks later, on June 18, Craft sought out William Wallace Cook, author of western adventure dime novels and dramas. He had already contacted Street & Smith, publisher of Cook's Buffalo Bill novels, about using his titles and stories. Craft asked Cook to write a few scenarios and promised he would talk to Cody for ideas.[19]

A few months later Panzer quit when his wife became ill, and Johnny Baker took over as director. Craft trusted Baker would be successful because "he understands stage management and is a conscientious and hard worker."[20] His confidence was well placed; the press compared Baker to David Belasco, a cutting-edge theater producer.[21] Cook sent some ideas, but Baker advised Craft of the near impossibility of creating complex scenes while the show was on the road. He suggested they film shorter segments and save the more spectacular staging for the off-season at the showmen's ranches. Cook came up with *Buffalo Bill's Test*, which was, according to Craft, "fine and just the thing that is needed as they should have no trouble in putting it on."[22] For his work, Cook, promised $35, received only $25, "which probably escaped from the film men in an unguarded moment."[23] Cody and Lillie became interested in the process and agreed to appear in all the scenes. By August, *Moving Picture World* reported that the photographer had already acquired several negatives.[24]

Meanwhile, Craft and Powers assured potential exhibitors that the showmen's fame guaranteed the film would be "a splendid drawing card." With anticipated release around September 15, the pictures might initially cost more, "but they would be a profitable investment."[25] Craft emphasized to *Moving Picture World* that this was no "lurid Western drama" but "a Biography of Nature's Nobleman, Enacted Personally by the Hon. Wm. F. Cody." He advertised the 3,000-foot documentary as *Buffalo Bill Bids You Good-bye*, the "last chance to see the Old Scout . . . as presented in the Farewell Performances of the most wonderful exhibition ever presented to the public."[26]

When filmgoers had begun demanding ever-changing shows, the concept of any one exhibitor buying films outright from the manufacturer—where prices ranged from ten to twenty-five cents a foot—proved impractical. Several exhibitors banded together to form "exchanges." When the Cody film was ready for distribution, however, most national film exchanges rejected it. In an approach known as "roadshowing," Craft then booked theaters and arranged for publicity himself, much as exhibitors had done in the first years of cinema. Based on Cody's popularity in Europe, the two partners also offered the screen rights to European exhibitors, hoping to sell rights for all European countries at one time.[27]

The online International Movie Database (IMDb) lists a Paul Panzer–directed film titled *The Life of Buffalo Bill* with professional actors William J. Craft, William V. Ranous, and Irving Cummings as cast members.[28] Reputable film historian Terry Ramsaye asserts that there were no dramatic scenes from 1910, "the only usable film was that portion of Col. Cody's story devoted to the Wild West show."[29] Managers at IMDb accept submissions from volunteer researchers, but no formal system is in place for authentication. Identification of actors in early twentieth-century films is suspect at best. In March 1917, *Motion Picture World* published a biographical article titled "The Actor in the Early Days," written by Panzer in first person. According to the article, he began his film career in 1905 with the Edison Company, then worked successively for Vitagraph, his own Pantograph Corporation, and the Pathé Brothers. In 1914 he starred in *The Perils of Pauline* and in *Jimmie Dale, Alias the Grey Seal*. It is likely that, if Panzer had been hired to direct a film starring such a world-renowned person as Cody, he would mention it, but he did not.[30] According to IMDb, the cast also included Panzer's future costar Pearl White, an actress who worked for Patrick Powers's studio around this time. Though she made several films, neither of her two biographers mentions her work on a Cody film.[31]

Johnny Baker contended that they made the biographical film in connection with the Wild West show; that the picture was merely experimental and was not used commercially. Cody and Lillie agreed it would not be exhibited, and Baker remembers it being destroyed.[32] This, perhaps, is the film IMDb credits to Panzer's direction.

Pliny Craft eventually reassembled the Wild West show section of the film and offered it for states rights sale by the Apex Film Company, the easiest and most logical way to handle nationwide release. Under the "states rights" system, producers sold their films to an individual or small company with rights to exhibit in a specific territory. The buyer then profited from whatever the market would bear. For feature film distribution, however, it was lucrative only to the states rights buyers, leaving the film-maker's profit just what he received from the initial sale. Craft credited himself with originating the idea as a "necessary after-consideration" of filming Cody's Wild West.[33] Hyman Winik bought the states rights for California and opened the picture in San Francisco with much success. Joseph P. Collins owned the New York rights and loaned a print of the film to George C. Tilyou to exhibit at Steeplechase Park during the summer. Considering them worthwhile, Tilyou also purchased the New Jersey rights in order to exhibit the films at Atlantic City, and Craft and Powers went home with $50,000 dollars.[34]

In 1992, the Buffalo Bill Historical Center staff compiled extant scenes of this film. The first in the set of three runs approximately fourteen minutes. The camera sits squarely on the arena grounds at eye level and shows many of the same scenes as previous Wild West show films: Cody offering water to his horse, cowboys and cowgirls on horseback, and the Deadwood stage. The picture cuts to a demonstration of Cody shooting glass balls, followed by a scene of high-stepping ponies. An intertitle informs viewers that the next spectacle is "The buffalo, and the famous huntsman in pursuit of his native game." When five buffalo rush into the arena, the cameraman wielding his bulky camera finds it difficult to keep them in the shot. Cody rides out from behind a curtain in pursuit and, as the buffalo stampede around the arena, he shoots, his blanks creating large puffs of smoke and, doubtless, a great deal of noise. The Battle of Summit Springs reenactment follows, with "The Final Salute" of the entire company ending the program.

A gap in the film leads into a Wild West parade honoring the twenty-fifth wedding anniversary of Pawnee Bill and Mrs. Lillie on August 31, 1910. The scene segues to bronco busting. With no chutes, cowboys mount the steers as their companions hold the animals down with ropes. In the "U.S. Artillery and Cavalry Drill," horses pull cannons on caissons, then soldiers demonstrate military maneuvers. Other fearless riders circle the arena standing on running horses. A long sequence features "Devlin's Zouaves," a synchronized sixteen-man marching team. In the final shot, the camera pans the entire Wild West entourage as cowboys and cowgirls jostle each other, smile, and wave their hats.[35]

The next set of scenes, lasting about twenty minutes, begins with "A Grand Review" and includes more introductory scenes "wherein the Occident meets the Orient in Gorgeous Pageantry, Pomp, and Procession."[36] After the Indians and Rough Riders, Cody rides into the scene and sweeps off his hat. The camera pans the front row of Indians as they urge their horses past. Intertitles once again announce "The Old Deadwood Stage Coach" and the subsequent Indian attack.

After a set of Johnny Baker's shooting, unsegued scenes of cowboys and cowgirls dancing a quadrille on horses show the performance from a different angle behind a watching cowboy. In this shot, the camera is on slightly higher ground resulting in

In a contest of football on horseback, it's cowboys versus Indians of
the Wild West show. (Buffalo Bill Museum and Grave, Lookout
Mountain, Golden, Colo.)

a better overview. Next on the program is "Foot Ball on Horseback, Indians vs. Cowboys." Both teams attempt to score by using
their horses to push a ball about six feet in diameter through goal-
posts. In another "Final Salute," the camera, again mounted high,
pans the scene as Cody reviews a final parade around the arena.[37]

A narrative scenario—"Pioneer events in Frontier days.
Indian life in Reality. Struggle in Conquering the Continent"—
introduces the Sioux. Dressed in native clothing, they are engaged
in making camp, trailing an enemy, and preparing for war when
their scouts spot a train of ox-drawn prairie schooners. That night,
after making camp, "happy that no sign of the enemies has been
discovered by the outriders," the travelers relax, dancing a quadrille on horseback. One Indian watches until he is certain the

settlers are oblivious to his presence. An Indian attack on the wagon train and a "realistic Indian battle scene as it actually occurred on the plains" conclude the scene.

Reviews indicated that this series of films "proved to be a great drawing card." Audiences at Happyland Theater in Auburn, New York, for instance, applauded after each reel, leading the town's newspaper editor to believe they "were surely satisfied."[38]

But Buffalo Bill Cody and Pawnee Bill Lillie were not.

CHAPTER 4

A Cinematic Biography

There is only one Buffalo Bill. For thirty years his name has been a drawing card all over the world. When he is gone these pictures will have to take his place.

MOVING PICTURE WORLD, MAY 4, 1912

Because Americans believed Cody really planned to retire soon, show profits at the end of the 1910 season reached $400,000. Encouraged by the numbers, the two Bills decided to carry on for another year.[1] While Lillie deposited his profits in a personal account and bought a new home on Oklahoma's Blue Hawk Peak, Cody poured his share into an Arizona mining company. Hoping for gold, he found tungsten which, while valuable for use in light bulbs, was not plentiful enough to make the mine lucrative.[2] Cody told a friend that his money woes forced him to smoke two-cent cigars and wear last year's clothes. He grew nervous from the "hard work and [was] sweating blood to meet all demands." He complained of having to enter the arena exhausted.[3]

Once he pondered, "Wouldn't it be great if a fellow had a good gold mine, so that when he needed more money all he would have to do would be to sen[d] some miners down in the mines and bring it up." Lillie reminded him the Wild West show was just that. "She is the biggest and best gold mine you or I will

ever have. You know she has given you all your ranches, your
hotels, and in fact every thing you have," including, Lillie could
have added, problems.[4]

Before the next season began in April 1911, they were embroiled
in a lawsuit against printer Joseph Mayer over program costs for
the previous tour. Mayer argued that the exhibition tent had been
poorly lighted, that employees' salaries were reduced, capable
performers dismissed, "inferior talent" employed, and several
large cities, usually on the circuit, bypassed. This perception cost
them revenue when several businesses refused to pay for their
ads. Mayer denied owing the showmen $3,036 from the contrac-
tual $12,026 and instead claimed $10,000 in damages because
the showmen had promised the tour would be "up to the past
standards." New York Supreme Court Justice Samuel Seabury
required specifics of Mayer's accusations and likely dismissed
the suit when these were not forthcoming.[5]

Cody again found himself in court when, with the Mayer case
on hold, Pliny Craft instigated an action after disputes arose
among the partners. The result, in May 1911, was a more specific
contract resolving ambiguous details of the June 1910 agreement.
New stipulations required Cody and the Wild West performers
to "pose," that is, appear, in 500–700 feet of a proposed 3,000-
foot film, previous to or during the Chicago engagement in mid-
July. Craft was obliged to give not less than fifteen hours' notice
of the time and place where he desired to film, and the location
must not be more than two miles from the showground. When
filming was complete, any negatives over 3,000 feet would belong
to Craft and Powers doing business as the Buffalo Bill and Pawnee Bill Film Company and could be used in other pictures. In
addition, the film company was to produce no fewer than 950
feet of new film each month for five years. Craft would devote
his time and energy to the business and, with Powers, supply
the necessary filmmaking labor and materials. Keeping strict

accounts, they would pay the showmen one third of the profits after expenses. Cody and Lillie were to pose "in any reasonable manner suitable," but neither was responsible for any failure in the filmmaking process. Finally, the contract forbade them to pose for, or to lend their names in connection with, any other film, a proviso Cody came to regret allowing.[6]

The 1911 Wild West season began with a bang, but Cody faced tough competition from the Millers when they deliberately played towns on the circuit before him, thereby diminishing audience interest in another western show. Philadelphia proved the exception, and Cody realized nearly $70,000 for the week. That was the last of the good times. A train wreck near Lowell, Massachusetts, in May and continuous inclement weather soon left the Wild West show "loosing money in every town." Cody complained, "I never seen New England so bad as now." After the Fourth of July, business continued to be so depressed, "we had lost back about $40,000.00."[7]

Discouraged and not always feeling well, he knew, "Should I miss a performance the newspapers would take it up then no one would come. Heaven knows we are loosing enough as it is."[8] General business manager Louis Cooke attempted to put a positive spin on the situation and reiterated for the *New York Clipper* Cody's entitlement to eventual retirement so "younger men can fill the saddle, enact the scenes, endure the elements and take the chances which he has not shirked in a most eventful career."[9]

Meanwhile, Craft and Powers continued their plan to film Cody's life in a popular format known as a biopic—a film covering the life of a real person. In July they offered twenty-six-year-old John B. O'Brien the opportunity to direct the feature-length film. At the time they lured him away from Essanay, O'Brien was specializing in villainous roles and doubled as business manager for Gilbert Anderson.[10] Familiar with the western lifestyle as well as the construction of western drama, O'Brien also knew his way around a movie camera.

Moving Picture World credits O'Brien with producing high-quality work under difficult circumstances. Filming took place while the Wild West was on tour, so he had to cope continually with changing locations. His most challenging task was getting the "polyglot assemblage" of Indians, cowboys, and Mexicans to produce some "intelligent action." They worked only reluctantly and regarded any extra action as worthy of extra pay.[11] At summer's end, O'Brien wrote to fellow Essanay actor Fred Church offering him a job as superintendent of the studio staff at Pawnee, Oklahoma. "As the concern is rated at two million," it would be good for him to get in on it soon.[12]

Two years earlier, *Moving Picture World* had sounded "A Note of Warning" for filmmakers, claiming that, in any thousand feet of film, "it is desirable to insure that it has plenty of action, and, moreover, that the dramatic interest is sustained and cumulative."[13] O'Brien made sure *The Life of Buffalo Bill* contained the requisite action.

The film opens with Cody riding through a stream in a wooded area, perhaps scouting for Indians or wildlife. His actual presence at the beginning and conclusion validates the film's claims of authenticity, as do the intertitles labeling the narrative as Cody's memories. In the first scene, "The Colonel Takes a Holiday," Cody rides up to the camera, rifle in hand, alone in the wilderness. Even without identification, there is no doubt that this is Buffalo Bill. Earlier in 1911 he had won a lawsuit against the Yankee Film Company, whose movies featured a "long-haired goateed figure in tasseled buckskin." The New York Supreme Court recognized that "Buffalo Bill has a sort of copyright on goatees of the peculiar form and color that adorns his chin."[14]

Shielding his eyes with his hand, Cody looks around. A modern critic commented on the "characteristic theatricality of Cody's poses. . . . [He] looks more like an actor from the Victorian stage

Cody scouts for Indians or wildlife in *The Life of Buffalo Bill*. (Buffalo Bill Historical Center, Cody, Wyo., video no. 427)

than an actual frontier hero."[15] Considering that Cody began his dramatic career as an untrained novice whom stage managers had literally to push onstage, his carryover of exaggerated actions from stage to film is reasonable. So too, such larger-than-life facial expressions and arm and hand movements carried the Wild West's story to arena audiences. In a clearing, he dismounts and removes his horse's saddle, then sits on the horse blanket to nap. A title announces "A Dream of the Days of His Youth."

Employing the dream or flashback format in theater and film enables storytellers to escape the rationality of waking hours and to use unorthodox editing or trick photography. As the focus of the action, the dreamer watches his own creation, which does not need to follow the dictates of logic. By 1912, filmmakers were making use of such techniques fairly regularly as a way to probe a character's psyche. In *The Life of Buffalo Bill*, O'Brien could have a young "Cody" performing the heroics of a young man without the elder real Cody actually doing them.[16] To accomplish this, in the longer middle section an actor in black wig takes the role of a younger Cody, beginning with "Memories of the Old Santa Fe Trail—The Way to the West Before the Railroad Came."

At "Sundown," a title card notifies the viewers, pioneers in a wagon train begin to set up camp and soon it is "Night on the plains." Nearby, Indians watch as Cody prepares a fire, then readies his horse for sleep. At "Sun Up Morning on the Plains," six "Indian Scouts Discover the Caravan" undetected at night, and they dive into a ravine to avoid being seen. The settlers scatter at "The Attack," but "Buffalo Bill Suprises [*sic*] the Indian Scouts" and kills two before they can harm anyone. As the others retreat, Cody approaches the wagon train to warn of a probable Indian return. The settlers stack saddles to hide behind.

The Indian scouts ride into their camp to report the deaths of their fellows. After dancing, "The Cheyennes Ready to Do Battle to Avenge Their Tribe," then ride across the plain in front of the stationary camera. The settlers succeed in driving them off. The number of females in the wagon train varies, something a modern continuity editor would ensure did not occur.

In "Another Memory of the Past," "Buck McCandell Arrives at Tonys and Plans to Hold up the Stage Coach" in scenes reminiscent of Cody's presentation of "The Great Train Hold-up." In a white shirt, broad white hat, and bandana, Buck enters a building identified by a corner sign as "Tonys." Five more men arrive on the scene and, when the stagecoach drives up, they wave it off.

Then "Buck McCandells Follows the Coach."

"Buffalo Bill learns that Buck McCandells has just Left and Follows." Cody comes upon the "The Rendezvous of the Bandits" and "He Discovers the Outlaws Scheme to hold up the Stage." Cody spots the stagecoach being pursued by the would-be robbers. He follows with rifle held high.

Buck McCandells arrives at Tony's. (Buffalo Bill Historical Center, Cody, Wyo., video no. 427)

In the next scene, "Buffalo Bill Gets Reinforcements" at Tony's, then, "In Pursuit of Buck McCandells, the Notorious Bandit," Cody leads his posse across the plains with, at first, four men. At next count there are six. As the stagecoach continues on over a ridge, Cody achieves "The Capture of the Bandits." McCandells and his gang raise their arms high in surrender.

Intertitles precede the film's third section: "Buffalo Bill with General Carr of the 5th Cav., U.S.A." It is 1876 again and, in full headdresses, "The Cheyennes Leaving to Join the Sioux" stream in front of the camera. "Buffalo Bill Discovers the Cheyennes," rides onto the scene from behind camera left, and dismounts to watch them. Afterward, he rides to Carr's camp and describes their location by drawing a map on the ground with a stick. He stands so far to camera left, however, that he is almost off screen. Cody and the officers mount up as a line of soldiers stand ready.

The Indians ride around in a circle demonstrating "Cheyennes Covering Their Trail," but Cody, Carr, and the soldiers approach from behind them. Both factions watch as Cody and an actor representing Yellow Hair (or Hand) circle each other, until Cody stabs him in "The Famous Duel between Chief Yellow Hand and Buffalo Bill Which Prevented the Cheyennes from Joining the Sioux." Indians and soldiers mill around, ostensibly unaware of the importance of the moment when Cody takes the "First Scalp for Custer." He holds aloft the Indian's headdress as the others ride off.

Finally, "Buffalo Bill Awakens from His Dream," rises, and saddles his horse. With his long white hair, Cody, moving slowly but still looking fit, circles his lasso, cinches his horse's saddle, and that's The End.

Clearly, many scenes came straight out of Wild West show scenarios. Cody taking Yellow Hand's (Hair's) scalp had been part of his theatrical exhibition since July 1876. He continued to exploit the event in the Wild West arena, but the novelty of having a younger "Cody" play himself proved impractical without benefit of an explanatory address to prevent audience confusion. The film survives, thanks in part to Blackhawk's 1959 editing of the 35 mm film from the George Kleine collection, Library of Congress. Blackhawk found the original to be "heavy and slow moving" in spite of the pre-1920s moviemakers' penchant for a plenitude of short quick scenes. But, even after the removal of long unchanging shots, critics continued to deride the film and O'Brien's direction.[17] Several cinematic techniques were leftovers from stage productions, such as the hand shielding the eyes. Some gaffes simply could have been refilmed to improve the final product, like centering the men when Cody maps out the Indians' location. In that scene, the camera never moves, so the action is framed as though it were a stage production: unidentified men stand to the right, a "chorus line" of soldiers forms a backdrop, and excessive sky and foreground frame the top and bottom of the screen.

Shots of the real Cody preparing to nap and then awakening bookend the film. It is noteworthy that two more sets of "book-ends" also appear. Critic Corey Creekmur, who found the film "unremarkable and even rather disappointing," noted the signifi-cance of two intertitles identifying the bulk of the film as a dream while two others inside the dream call the scenes memory.[18] When Cody awakens and rises, it appears he is off to repeat the events he dreamed or remembered. *Moving Picture World* praised O'Brien's success "in making this picture after two other directors had failed," possibly referring to Pliny Craft's and Paul Panzer's attempts.[19]

By 1912, having been in the public eye for forty years, Cody was recognizable through dime novels, theatrical productions, and the Wild West show, as well as his actual newsworthy feats. As a result, viewers attended the film with a preconceived notion of its content based on the title. They may have been aware that Cody was now too old to replicate the daring deeds of his past, but he did do them. Promotions reminded patrons that in many movie houses management advertised hour-long shows, but these con-sisted of ten minutes of advertising slides, ten more minutes spent rewinding and adjusting the reels, and only forty minutes of film. But the "Actual moving pictures by Cody, Himself" were over two hours long, thereby supplying "more for the money."[20] To exhibi-tors, a promotion touted "A STATE RIGHTS OFFER OF GREAT VALUE, Having the added drawing power of a name popular everywhere." The Buffalo Bill and Pawnee Bill Film Company would provide an assortment of lithographed posters by the Courier Company of Buffalo, New York, and also promised to "furnish a Surety Bond for $1,000 to every purchaser against invasion of territory."[21]

Poster for *The Life of Buffalo Bill* highlighting the "First Scalp for Custer." (Courtesy of Tony Sapienza, DMD, Ridgewood, N.J.)

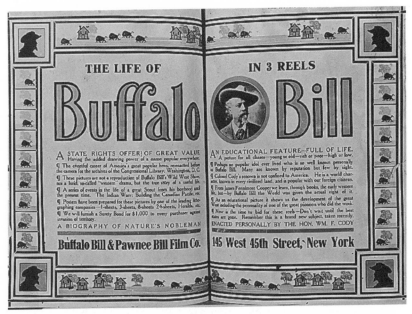

Movie ad, *Moving Picture World*, May 4, 1912.

Another ad in *Moving Picture World* enticed exhibitors with the conviction that "this set of pictures [is] an investment that will be earning dividends for years.[22]

> Why? Because they perpetuate a great personality. A character that is indelibly identified with American History. The older they grow the more valuable they become. Some day they will be priceless.
>
> An educational feature with all the thrill of real Western life. A truthful record of the life of the only surviving hero of the Indian Wars. Colonel Cody is the last of a vanishing type of pioneer who passed into history before the invention of Motography.
>
> There is only one Buffalo Bill. For thirty years his name has been a drawing card all over the world. When he is gone these pictures will have to take his place.

Joseph Gandos, a buyer for three states, reported that the biopic played to record-breaking houses. He encouraged teachers to arrange for their pupils to see it after school and made special arrangements with lecturers to introduce the biography in the evening. Walter Barnsdale, a Wisconsin exhibitor, promoted the film as "the best Wild West picture subject ever made, and a far better performance than Cody ever gave in the circus arena." How Cody took the backhanded compliment is not known.[23]

Cody hoped such incentives worked because, with show expenses continually rising, he needed the money. In May 1912 a vaudeville firm offered him $3,000 a week to appear with the film. Because their contract forbade such competition, Cody and Lillie applied for an injunction restraining Powers and Craft from using the picture and asked for their share of the proceeds. The suit charged that, according to the June 1910 contract, Craft and Powers had the right to display "small moving picture plays of Western scenes" with the showmen receiving $25,000 and a percentage of the profits. When payments were not forthcoming, the showmen refused to act any more. In retaliation, the Buffalo Bill and Pawnee Bill Film Company, namely, Craft and Powers, sued them for $1,000,000. Cody and Lillie then claimed that the 8,000 feet of film Powers and Craft had placed on the market under the name of the Buffalo Bill and Pawnee Bill Film Company would diminish demand for future pictures they might make and even deprive them of profits to be made with the arena show. This was a reasonable possibility, particularly since admittance to the film of the Wild West show cost only ten cents, whereas entry to the arena show itself cost at least fifty cents. At the end of May, Justice James Gerard of the New York Supreme Court denied the showmen's motion.[24]

In reprisal, the Buffalo Bill and Pawnee Bill Film Company sued Lillie and Cody over articles in trade papers in which the showmen claimed they had not authorized the film whose rights Powers and Craft controlled worldwide. The move effectively intimidated exhibitors from buying and showing it. Again, Justice Gerard upheld the film company's claim to sole rights of the picture. In advertising the film thereafter, Craft and Powers stated that exhibitors and prospective state rights purchasers should not fear "molestation from outside parties," including, presumably, the showmen, for the company would stand by any transaction and would furnish a $1,000 bond against any "controversy."[25]

Not just another in the panoply of westerns, the film with Cody's name in the title as well as in the promotions capitalized on the emerging moving picture "star system." When Cody started his theatrical troupe in 1872, the "combination" was becoming a phenomenon in which theatrical companies took to the road with a starring actor in the drama's lead. With hundreds of melodramatic combinations touring the country in the 1870s through 1890s, theater managers based their scheduling on the star's appeal and earning capacity. Similarly, early motion picture actors were generally anonymous until audiences began to demand knowledge of their names and lifestyles. Enterprising businessmen found a ready market for movie magazine tell-alls, like *Movie Pictorial* or *Motion Picture Album*, that catered to the public's demand. For the producer, this was good and bad news. Named stars sustained cinematic interest, but the more highly charged their names, the more they could demand in salary. To keep production costs down, a producer had to entice exchanges to order more films on a regular basis.

Defeated in the courts, but still hoping the films would generate enough profit for retirement, Cody wrote his cousin Frank, "I am trying to get out of the show business. . . . I am compelled to work sick or well and at 67 its harder to pull myself together than it was 30 years ago."[26] He tried to deny that his show celebrated an era and locale fast becoming only a memory. As early as 1896, the press hit the target as precisely as Cody's marksmanship: "Standing as the connecting link between the past and the present, [Buffalo Bill] draws back the curtain of retrospection and reveals the picturesque figures who played dramatic parts in the border life of American history. Buffalo Bill's Wild West show is a living picture of other days."[27] The myth of the West Cody celebrated would live on, but the profitable days of cowboys and Indians running through their stunts for an arena audience were nearing an end. Filmmakers copied his invention and style, even his particular grooming and dress. So, how much longer could his Wild West show withstand the inexorable competition of the movies?

CHAPTER 5

Disaster in Denver

It was wonderful and pathetic . . .
FRANK BALDWIN, *DENVER POST*, AUG. 25, 1913

When all was said and done, the 1912 Wild West season showed
receipts for only $125,000. In December the United States Printing
and Lithograph Company, holding $16,000 worth of Cody's
notes maturing in April and May 1913, contracted to print posters
and programs for the next season at an additional $50,000. Cody
was already short of cash needed to keep the show in winter
quarters. Previously Lillie had advanced him his share, taking it
out of the season's profits, but he asked Cody to pay his half for
1912. Cody could spare only $15,000 but promised to remit the
balance later.[1]

In late January 1913, Cody was guest of honor at the Colorado
Commandery Military Order of Foreign Wars annual dinner.[2]
In Denver he met two of the most notoriously shrewd and unscrupulous men he would ever encounter. A biographer identified
Frederic G. Bonfils and Harry H. Tammen, respectively, as a
"past-master of mean grafters" and a man who "enjoyed nothing
quite so much as seeing a sucker squirm."[3] With Bonfils putting
up the money and Tammen supplying the brains, the pair had

collaborated to buy Denver's "piddling little" *Evening Post* and turned it into the prosperous *Denver Post.* They also bought a dog and pony show, united it with circus acts as the Sells-Floto Circus, and competed zealously with Barnum & Bailey and the Ringling Brothers.

Cody mentioned his pressing need for cash, and the two circled much as lions might ambush a wounded gazelle. In exchange for a $20,000 loan, Cody pledged his services and lent his name to their circus, using the Lillie-owned Wild West show as collateral. Under the January 28 agreement, Cody was to travel with Sells-Floto beginning in 1914, manage its Wild West feature, and appear in parades for 40 percent of receipts over $3,000.[4]

The *Denver Post* proclaimed it "the most important deal ever consummated in American amusement enterprise." The "Buffalo Bill Exposition of Frontier days and the Passing of the West" would be "preserved, added to, and given with the circus performance." What Tammen wanted was Cody—minus Lillie—lock, stock, and barrel, and he got him. Because of the complicated financial machinations, Cody either did not realize he was selling his name and services or assumed the contract would be void once he repaid the debt.[5] When Lillie questioned the move, Cody assured him he had done nothing to interfere with their show, but upon learning the whole story Lillie became livid. He had sufficient funds to pay their creditors, but now Cody had signed a deal to cut him out for a rival concern.[6] A few days later, Cody left for Canada, but he became too ill in London, Ontario, to speak at the unveiling of a monument erected by the Daughters of the American Revolution commemorating the Pony Express. He had not recovered by his sixty-seventh birthday on February 26.[7]

Modernizing the Wild West show for the 1913 season with a demonstration of automobile polo that combined "motor races, flying machines, daredevil driving and speed contest" did little to entice audiences.[8] The show fared badly when cold, rainy weather kept crowds away. From Tennessee, Cody, ill once again, admitted to his sister: "I am not at all strong. . . . Worry has broken my once iron constitution. . . . This is a Killing life." At times he did not appear in his familiar buckskins upon his horse but wore a frock suit and drove an open barouche into the arena. Soon he had all but abandoned the saddle. Despite poor attendance, he assured a reporter that people supported western shows as well as in the past, saying, "The country is in a very prosperous condition, and as long as the American has money in his pockets he will patronize a show providing the performance offered is a good one."[9]

By June he was suffering nervous exhaustion and stomach trouble. Reporters began to speculate that he was dying, but the old showman refuted the gossip: "The newspapers think its up to them to kill me off every little while. During the Indian wars they killed me about once a month now about three times a year. But I am still Kicking."[10]

In early July, Chicago's extreme heat contributed to low attendance, a devastating adjunct to the Printing and Lithograph Company's threat of foreclosure. They had supplied advertisements per agreement but had received no payment. General counsel for the company, Adolph Marks, was told to attach the show but, not wanting to embarrass Cody, was reluctant to do so.[11] As the show traveled throughout the Midwest, a representative of the printing company warned Lillie not to take the show to Denver, Tammen's home turf, because he would certainly foreclose on it. The *Denver Post* was already predicting that the Sells-Floto Circus would become the "Finest and Largest Organization of Its Kind When Joined Next Year by Buffalo Bill's Show," inadvertently prophesying that "there never was anything like Buffalo Bill's Wild West show before; there never will be anything like it again."[12]

Heedless of the warning, on July 21 the showmen paraded the Wild West to Denver's Union Park. History shows the city was a town of conclusions for Cody, where he had voluntarily disbanded his theatrical troupe in April 1886; he would die within its gates in 1917. It was also about to become the last city to see an appearance of his Wild West show. For a change, Cody was feeling well, looking like a "truly grand old fellow with the flowing white hair and the iron, dauntless face . . . as erect, alert and full of 'go' as if the sixty-seven years of all sorts of vicissitudes had not been lived through."[13]

But the next day proved disastrous. Given no choice, the printing company attached the Wild West show for nonpayment. Marks offered credit for two years if Lillie would transfer the mortgages he held on Cody's North Platte ranch and Irma Hotel. Lillie refused. After the printing company's action, the two Denver newsmen had no choice but to also attach to protect their loan. As a businessman, Lillie realized it was time to cut his losses and fled to New Jersey to file a bankruptcy petition, but Denver attorneys had earlier filed a petition for involuntary bankruptcy.

Denver attorneys Charles Redmond and John Bottom, representing the lithograph company, handled the attachment, claiming the show and its railroad cars, even tracks on which the cars stood. In on all of the meetings, the attorneys were also legal advisers to the *Post* and almost certainly kept Tammen and Bonfils apprised of every aspect of negotiations.[14]

Although Marks, Tammen, and Bonfils insisted that they were not out to embarrass Cody, from his point of view they had. A week later his signed letter appeared in the *Denver Post* explaining that he had borrowed money expecting to repay it, but "our losses were large and constant." Nearly all the performers had been placed with other amusement enterprises, Cody reported. "I am glad to make this statement in justice to Messrs. Tammen and Bonfils, because, during the entire matter they have been unusually kind, indulgent and generous." One reason Cody may have felt kindly toward them came to light three years later in the case of *Bonfils and Tammen v. Buffalo Bill's Wild West and*

Pawnee Bill's Great Far East Combined. Cody testified that, after the attachment, Tammen told him he and Bonfils would not hold him personally liable for the note and that it had been paid. After all, Cody said, he never personally borrowed the $20,000, it was for the corporation.[15]

After a federal judge set a date for the show to be sold at auction, attorneys assessed show properties and made preparations. In all, three separate auctions on August 21, August 27, and September 15 were necessary to dispose of Wild West property. Cody seems to have kept out of the hoopla. What bothered him most was the auctioning of his favorite horse, Isham. It appeared that his friends bid against each other to own the horse that had been Cody's when, in fact, they each bid with the intent of returning the horse to him.

Cody appeared optimistic about his future in public. The *North Platte Telegraph* reported him saying, "I am not down and out but just starting life. . . . although I regret the scandal and publicity this gives me in the end it will be the best." Nevertheless, he revealed his true feelings to a friend: "The old show went out of business on the 22d it nearly broke my heart. . . . I am going off into the rockies for a little mental and bodly rest. . . . I am not down and out by a long Jump."[16]

In Cody, Buffalo Bill planned his next move instead of seizing the opportunity to retire. He suspected that one factor contributing to his problems was "imitations of his Wild West show that flooded the country in recent years and by their very tawdriness detracting from the fame of the real thing."[17] Even as he complained that competition from movies, especially westerns, also hurt his business, a New York film company contacted him to suggest that he do a Wild West picture.[18]

The prospect kindled an idea. Instead of partnering with the likes of Pliny Craft in role-playing a fictional plot or in a moving picture that merely recorded scenes from his Wild West show, Cody decided to film his true-life experiences with the army and the Indians. Though his part was significant, he was but one of many outstanding men who had aided in the "advance of white civilization," and he became convinced "that each of the few survivors while still able to do so Should tell the plain unvarnished history of the March of Civilization west of the Missouri river." He had been told, "We owe it not only to the present but future generations."[19] One line of Turner's 1893 thesis resonated with him. Throughout America's history, "fall lines" marked the stages of the frontier: the Allegheny mountains, Mississippi and Missouri rivers, the desert, the Rockies, and finally California. "Each was won by a series of Indian wars," Turner had written.[20] This Cody knew well. He decided to make it the theme of his film.

Wild West programs had recapped the "touchingly pathetic" story of American Indians, who were slowly but surely "passing from our gaze forever."[21] With one more chance to tell the story, it could be Cody's legacy, his final presentation of the settlement of the West. He may have read reports in *Moving Picture World* calling for "Accuracy in Indian Subjects": "Pictures of that kind are what we need . . . as they are of much value to those seeking knowledge on such subjects." He probably also knew of Indians who staged an "uprising" against "grossly libelous" movies that used whites costumed as Indians.[22] Cody valued authenticity and was convinced he could faithfully preserve events in the country's western history through the medium of moving pictures.

He had always had an uncanny knack for being in the right place at the right time. Film historian David Robinson calls the year 1913 a watershed, and so it proved to be, not only for Cody but for the entire movie industry. New film companies were emerging daily and soon headed west from the eastern seaboard. With the world war inhibiting production and import of European films, American movies proliferated in an ever-growing market. Interest in film stars fueled the appeal and improved techniques in filming and production enhanced the variety of cinematic topics demanded by more sophisticated audiences. It was a good time to get into the business.[23]

Cody was ready and decided on three outstanding battles to portray: Summit Springs, Warbonnet Creek, and Wounded Knee. Each would feature not only the Indians but himself as the star and would reveal the complicated machinations involved in the long series of Indian wars. He could highlight his involvement in military strategy and once again tell of his daring deeds. Western films offered ample opportunities for a gallant hero, and what greater heroic actions than Cody's own in the Indian wars?

On July 11, 1869, he had been acting as Gen. Eugene A. Carr's Fifth Cavalry's chief of scouts. Earlier in the summer, Cheyenne chief Tall Bull and his renegade band had conducted vengeful raids on the borders of Nebraska and Kansas after failed parleys with military leaders over the desolate quality of their reservation. Their kidnapping of two Kansas women was the last straw for army commander Gen. Philip Sheridan, who ordered the Fifth to find the Indians, recapture the women, and "pursue and punish those Indians no matter where they go."[24]

Following their trail, Cody located the Indian camp. When Carr's troops surprised the village at Summit Springs, Colorado, they found one kidnapped woman dead and the other nearly so. Tall Bull with twenty others rode to a ravine and watched as the army's Pawnee scouts surrounded him. He raised his head and fired. In the midst of the ensuing battle, it is difficult to say whose return fire actually killed the warrior. Over the years, Carr revised his report several times, alternately crediting Sgt. Daniel McGrath, an unidentified Pawnee, Lt. George Mason, and Cody as the slayer. In Cody's version, of course, *he* shot Tall Bull, and his reenactment of the event in the Wild West show was easily its "most imposing feature."[25]

An incident from the Great Sioux War would feature as the film's second conflict. Three weeks after the fall of Lt. Col. George A. Custer and his Seventh Cavalry on June 25, 1876,

Cody was again in position as chief scout for the Fifth when troopers encountered Cheyennes heading north to join Sitting Bull's Sioux. Col. Wesley Merritt's troops expected to confront them at Warbonnet Creek and set up an ambush. Cody noticed a dozen Cheyennes breaking off from the main band and suggested that he and a handful of scouts head them off. When Gen. Charles King gave the order, Cody and his companions crossed the creek. As they drew near the small group led by Yellow Hair, both men fired at once. Cody's shot pierced Yellow Hair's leg. The Indian's shot missed, but Cody's second shot killed him as his cohorts fled. A minute after the first shot, the remainder of the troopers dashed past Cody, who was standing over the body. General King, watching the event from a short distance away, remembered Cody "waving the handsome war bonnet and shouting something—perhaps it is, 'First Scalp for Custer.'"[26]

In later years, his nemeses claimed it was not Cody who killed the Cheyenne and that the scalp came from some other Indian. Another yarn spread that Yellow Hair specifically challenged him. They circled each other, pistols and knives ready. A deadly hand-to-hand struggle ensued until finally Cody plunged his knife into his opponent. General King tried to correct the hearsay, but when Cody returned to the stage his drama chronicled the more sensational version. King recalled Cody eventually admitting he had played that "fool piece of fiction so long he believed it himself."[27]

The last of Cody's Indian wars depictions would give credence to Ernest Thompson Seton's observation that "all massacres of Indians by the whites were accomplished by treachery *in times of peace*, while all Indian massacres of whites were *in time of war*, to resist invasion."[28]

The battle at Wounded Knee had taken place only twenty years previously, not so long ago for survivors to have forgotten the horror. The confrontation resulted from the government's reaction to the Sioux Ghost Dance, which was the Indians' justifiable

Cody reenacts taking the "first scalp for Custer." (Buffalo Bill Museum and Grave, Lookout Mountain, Golden, Colo.)

reaction to government policy. By the 1880s, in an attempt to force the tribes to assimilate, regulations had confined nearly all tribes on land so poor no white person would want it. Promised rations and supplies were likewise of poor quality, rotten and inedible, if they arrived at all. Experienced Indian fighter Lt. Gen. Nelson A. Miles recognized that the government's lack of adherence to treaties was a major factor causing the uprisings.[29]

The time was propitious for a cause uniting Indians against whites. When Paiute spiritual leader Wovoka announced his messianic mission to prepare Indians for salvation, tribes from all over the plains sent representatives to learn from him. He taught a nonviolent Ghost Dance and prophesied that, through the Indians' singing and dancing, the whites would return to Europe from where they came. Buffalo would return to the plains, and peaceful Indians would live with the ghosts of their ancestors.

Kicking Bear and his brother-in-law Short Bull visited Wovoka during the summer of 1890. On his return, Kicking Bear called on Sitting Bull and told him all he had learned, but he gave the lessons a more fatalistic interpretation in which sweet grass would grow over the land and bury all white men. If the Indians just wore the holy shirts and sang the songs, he preached, any soldiers who might come after them would drop dead; others would run.

As the number of Indians involved increased, so did the Indian agents' panic. At first Sitting Bull endorsed the dance, but he became fearful when it made some Indian agents nervous enough to call in the military.[30]

Agent James McLaughlin at Standing Rock wondered why the dancing alarmed authorities. The Sioux were poor and weak, in no condition to revolt. In a letter to Indian Affairs commissioner T. J. Morgan, he expressed disgust at newspaper reports causing unnecessary alarm among nearby settlers.[31] Though the Indians showed no inclination to fight, McLaughlin conceded that the dancing had stirred them up, so he removed Kicking

Bear from Standing Rock and advised him not to practice the new religion. Short Bull headed with Chief Big Foot's people to the Dakota Badlands, where they circled around a central tree and danced until they collapsed.

In Chicago, General Miles, commander of the Military Division of the Missouri, considered the situation critical but controllable. He could find no objections to the dancing, believing the movement would, as Chief Red Cloud at Pine Ridge had said, "disappear as the snow before the heat of the sun." Having no intention to subvert Wovoka's message into a military action, Short Bull also couldn't understand the hostility. "We had no thought of fight; if we had meant to fight, would we not have carried arms? We went unarmed to the dance. How could we have held weapons? For thus we danced, in a circle, hand in hand, each man's fingers linked in those of his neighbor."[32]

Watching the goings-on from Europe, Cody, who had befriended Sitting Bull in 1885 when the chief traveled with the Wild West show, felt that dealing with him was a move toward settlement of the troubles. "Of all the bad Indians, Sitting Bull is the worst," Cody believed, but he was ambivalent about his role if the situation should evolve into another Indian/army battle. "I don't know yet whether I shall fight them or not," he said at the time. "It might not look exactly right for me to do so, for I have made a fortune out of them."[33] The potential for glory in yet another military conflict resolved his indecision. When Cody returned to the states for a government inquiry into his treatment of the show Indians, Miles summoned him to convince Sitting Bull to "drop the agitation" and come in off the reservation to be arrested. With no further hesitation, in late November 1890, Cody headed for Indian country.[34]

Furious at General Miles's decision, McLaughlin ordered Cody sidetracked when he arrived and petitioned Washington to rescind the orders. After deliberation, President Harrison ordered him to return. Cody told a reporter, "We could have taken the Bull, horse and all into captivity, I am sure, without the loss of a single life."[35]

But this was not the case. In early December, Brig. Gen. Frank Baldwin met with Miles about Cody's aborted attempt. Finally convinced of the potential for danger, Miles viewed repression of the Ghost Dance as an opportunity to "demonstrate the continued importance of strong military in the western United States." Meanwhile, McLaughlin had ordered Sitting Bull's arrest, believing him to be the power behind the Ghost Dance. Some Indian police entered his cabin as a crowd of his well-armed supporters gathered outside. Without warning, someone's rifle discharged, triggering a barrage of shots. Dozens of Indians died in minutes, among them Sitting Bull.[36]

Two weeks later, on December 28, 1890, Chief Big Foot was leading his band of Miniconjous from the Cheyenne River reservation to the Pine Ridge agency to surrender. They had participated in the Ghost Dance, so were deemed "hostile" when the Seventh Cavalry intercepted them. Col. James Forsyth had orders to disarm the band before escorting them farther. When the request for arms yielded few, he ordered a search. Warriors resisted and, during the search, a shot was discharged. Nervous soldiers retaliated; the Sioux, in turn, fought with the little they had. Fear, nervousness, and blind rage fueled unstoppable chaos. Soldiers fired indiscriminately on the Indians with rapid-firing Hotchkiss guns positioned on the surrounding hills. General Miles's understated report says it all: "A general melée and massacre occurred, in which a large number of men, women, and children were killed and wounded."[37]

Cody was present days later when Miles reviewed the troops. Benefiting his Wild West show, Miles, and the Indian authorities, Cody was permitted to recruit nearly one hundred Sioux, a quarter of them Ghost Dance prisoners, to travel with him for the

1891 season. But, in empathy, he never reenacted the Wounded Knee massacre in any performance.[38]

With unique knowledge gained from having worked closely with both factions, Cody hoped his proposed film would set the story straight and finally engender understanding, if not acceptance, of what had happened. He would forever regret his failure to bring in Sitting Bull peaceably and believed that, if Washington had allowed him to carry out his orders, the chief would have come without misfortune and there would have been no more trouble from the Sioux.[39] By signing the disciplined Indians to the Wild West cast, Cody saved them from military prison. Some army regiments had played a damning role, but Miles received credit for bringing about the allegiance of the surviving Indians. Neither Cody nor any of the generals took active part in the battle, but he would parlay his version of the confrontation into the major story of the film.

CHAPTER 6

Cue the Government, the Army, the Financiers

We'll do it, Bill. . . . You and I and General Miles will do it;
and posterity will be able to see that end of an epoch.
FRANK BALDWIN, *DENVER POST*, AUG. 25, 1913

With a plan in mind to bring the true history of the Indian wars to the movies, Cody needed three specifics to fall into place: government endorsement and permissions, financial assistance, and sanction of the participants.

He referred to Harry Tammen as "the man who had my show sold at sheriff sale which broke my heart."[1] Nevertheless, unable to acknowledge that Tammen and Frederic Bonfils had duped him, Cody asked them for backing. With bank loans hard to come by for new films and his own credit on the skids, Cody had no choice. "Go as far as you like, Bill," they both said, feeling generous after their Wild West coup. "We will finance you." That Cody had already received three enticing offers for a prospective film was incentive. Excited as a child at Christmas, Cody pressed on with the "ardor and energy of a young man of twenty-one." He wrote his son-in-law, "It looks like this is going to be a winner."[2]

Scarcely a week after the Wild West's attachment, Cody arrived in Wyoming, where his attendance at Cheyenne's Frontier Days brought the grandstand to its feet. "You don't know how good it makes me feel," he said, "just to be back here among all the boys again and see them work." He watched the exhibition "like the old buffalo bull driven out of the herd by the younger bucks."[3] When Secretary of Interior Franklin K. Lane arrived to inspect the Shoshone Irrigation Project, Cody, eager to get on with his cinematic project, spoke to him about employing Pine Ridge reservation Indians. To sweeten the proposition, Cody promised a reel showing the Indians' progress since their surrender in January 1891. The film would also prove the "excellent" treatment the U.S. government accorded the contemporary Indian and would be a record of the soon-to-be extinct tribes. Lane sanctioned the project on condition that Commissioner of Indian Affairs Cato Sells and Pine Ridge agent Maj. John R. Brennan approved as well.

On August 20, Secretary of War Lindley M. Garrison also visited Wyoming and dined at Cody's Pahaska lodge. Cody needed Garrison to authorize the participation of army cavalry units and so turned the conversation to the film, the progress of the Indian nations from the days of savagery to the present, and to Secretary Lane's interest.[4]

A few days later, Cody drove with Brig. Gen. Frank D. Baldwin to Fort Logan near Denver. Baldwin, as acting inspector general, had been on the Wounded Knee scene in 1891. When Cody asked him if he remembered that day, Baldwin averred, "As well as though it was yesterday." They talked of Baldwin's stationing six thousand U.S. troops and two thousand National Guard on one side of the ravine. Five thousand Indians, including women and children, had marched across it and stood facing them, ready to surrender.

"Years and years we had fought, general, battle after battle, to make that day possible and, somehow, as I watched them I felt the tears come into my eyes at this proof of the final defeat of such a foe."

"Great foes they were," agreed Baldwin, "and I felt as you did, Bill, about them. It was wonderful and pathetic . . . an end of an epoch."

Cody then told him of his "scheme . . . of great historical interest" to reproduce some of the last battles of the war with one thousand troops and five hundred Indians at the exact site.

"You would take part in it?"

"I would," said Cody.

"Well, then, so will I," said Baldwin and told Cody he would also ask General Miles.[5] When they reached the National Guard at Golden, Colorado, Secretary Garrison gave his permission for the Twelfth Cavalry stationed at Fort Robinson, Nebraska, to participate. The troops were not Indian fighters, but they were located nearest the Pine Ridge reservation. A world war was looming, and the *Denver Post* had quoted Garrison saying the United States was unprepared. The government, desperate for recruits, was willing "to establish a three-ring circus to attract them." He had acquiesced, realizing the film's potential for encouraging enlistments to a military full of "noble history." Given Cody's promise of authenticity, he also saw it as a permanent record for the War Department.[6]

There followed a flurry of consulting telegrams from Commissioner Sells to Major Brennan at Pine Ridge, and from Brennan to and from Secretary Lane. For the most part, Brennan could see no objection. He worried only about the effect on his charges, that the troops' presence might distress them. After all, Wounded Knee had occurred only a generation past. Cody swore his plan meant a "reunion of participants who are surviving and preserving for future generations of great events by aid of the camera" under Brennan's supervision. The Indians would not need to leave the reservation; furthermore, the film company would pay all expenses, including food.[7] Secretary Lane had still not fully committed, so a joint telegram from Bonfils and Cody stated optimistically that "the Reunion between the Indians and their old time enemies will be as amiable as the recent reunion at Gettysburg, in which opposing factions once engaged in bitterest hatred were brought to gether in a spirit of fine friendliness. . . . Everything will be done to insure the future generation a most worthy document of a great event, which has few of its distinguished participants left to tell the story."[8]

With Brennan and Sells on board, Lane also decided to sanction this "good thing, as the characters referred to are most of them old men, and this is about the last chance we will have to get a reproduction of what took place at Pine Ridge."[9]

With government approval secured, consideration of filmmaker came next. In late August, Cody and Tammen traveled to Chicago to talk to officers at Essanay, the filmmakers specializing in westerns since 1908. Advertising emphasized that their movies, made in the West amid genuine scenery, were a factor in their success. Cody probably felt right at home, passing through a doorway "flanked by the terra cotta heads of two Indians in colorful feathered headdresses, the studio's trademark." Essanay was a good choice; its president, George Spoor, the *Denver Post* disclosed, "taboos the vulgar and the cheap grade of pictures and leans to the educational, the patriotic and true to life." He was also a longtime fan of Cody, believing he "had more to do with the remarkable progress and development of the West than any other person."[10]

From Essanay's eleven traveling companies, Spoor assigned Vernon R. Day as production manager and Theodore Wharton as director. D. T. (David) Hargan was to do the actual filming, with Conrad Luperti as co-cinematographer, along with a corps of photographers and other cameramen. Essanay provided the cameras, film stock, and costumes. The Cody company would distribute the film using Essanay's Chicago address.[11] An experienced director/producer, Milwaukee-born Wharton first found work in the movies as a scriptwriter for Edison, with rapid promotions to editor and studio supervisor. At the Kalem company he established an indoor studio, then he became the first director at the Pathé brothers' American studio. He worked for Essanay for two years before taking on Cody's project. Wharton would need all of his training in the staging of the scenes, showing the inexperienced actors what to do and seeing that they could do it confidently before the cameras recorded the action. *Moving Picture World* observed the "enormous undertaking" ahead of him, for besides handling the troops, Indians, officers, and horses he would have to contend with Cody, who, the press warned, was something of a prima donna. Several other producers had attempted films with him, "but with indifferent results, mainly on this account."[12]

One of the final items on Cody's to-do list was securing the cooperation and support of General Miles, General King, and other former Indian fighters. As advisors on military affairs, uniforms, accoutrements, and strategy, their firsthand knowledge could greatly contribute to the film's accuracy. Throughout many years together in the field, Miles, in particular, had found in Cody a friend, and the feeling was mutual.

Forging an impressive army career based on bravery and determination, Miles had risen to the rank of general in spite of his "consuming ambition, over-aggressiveness, impatience, and self-opiniation." His biographer thought his great weakness was pride; Theodore Roosevelt pegged him as a "brave peacock."[13] Though Cody respected Miles as "the reincarnation of Napoleon," a clash between their two forceful personalities proved inevitable.[14] Miles had known Frank Baldwin for many years before Baldwin approached him with Cody's plan. He wondered briefly if the opportunity would allow him to manipulate past events to show himself and the army in a favorable light, but he replied, "If the parties are responsible and really desire to reproduce an important and historic event, in a truthful and accurate manner, then we could very properly assist them."[15] Although Miles was not present at any of the battles

Cody expected to film, as commanding officer he wielded control. He did not hesitate to inform reporters that his job was to ensure events would be filmed exactly as they had happened.

To write part of the screenplay, Cody chose Charles King, a West Pointer with wounds to prove his service under generals Crook and Miles in the Indian, Civil, and Spanish Wars. Cody and King were also old friends; they had hunted buffalo and served in the Fifth Cavalry together as part of the Big Horn expedition. Cody recalled him as a "splendid little officer, brave as a lion. Always volunteering for posts of danger and always ready to go to the front." After retiring, King turned to writing and had over fifty books on military and western history to his credit, as well as several novels.[16] Like Cody, King sympathized with American Indians' defense of their homes and lifestyle. He criticized government policies that disregarded treaties and ignored the actions of corrupt Indian agents. Selig Polyscope had bought the dramatic rights to several of King's novels and based some of its westerns on his stories. Attending military and western films kept him familiar with current trends in the movie industry. At a meeting in Chicago's La Salle hotel, Cody, Tammen, and Johnny Baker outlined the project and asked King to write the photoplay for the Yellow Hair encounter and Summit Springs battle.[17]

To round out the cadre of military officers who had participated in the original battles, Cody invited Maj. Gen. Jesse M. Lee, Miles's 1891 aide-de-camp Brig. Gen. Marion Maus, and Col. Horatio G. Sickel. At present commanding the Twelfth Cavalry, Sickel had been a young officer at Wounded Knee in 1890 and sketched the field at the time, a map that became a valuable asset to the filmmakers.[18]

With all of Cody's ducks in a row, on Monday, September 8, 1913, the Col. W. F. Cody (Buffalo Bill) Historical Pictures Company was incorporated under Colorado laws. Its officers were Bonfils, president; Cody, vice president; Spoor, treasurer; Tammen, secretary; and Day, assistant secretary. According to the contract,

Cody would receive one-third interest because he "possesses a store of information relating to the early settlement of the West, Indian battles, history and legends." Spoor's Essanay company owned a third interest for his understanding of the movie business and for the use of his facilities for film manufacture, and the remainder belonged to Bonfils and Tammen, whose expertise lay in publicity. The company would issue 120 shares of stock at $100 each. Spoor, Tammen, and Bonfils paid $6,000 into the treasury; Cody paid nothing, and when he spent time locating and setting the scenes the company paid his traveling and living expenses. Each partner gave one dollar to the others to bind the contract. All were exhorted to "devote as much of their time to the enterprise as they can consistently spare from their regular business," with no remuneration until the company proved solvent enough to pay dividends. With obvious eagerness, Cody confided to a friend: "These gentlemen are all millionaires and pretty good fellows to have as partners, as they furnish all the money. . . . I think I am in line here, at least all the moving picture people think so, to make a lot of money yet this winter."[19]

The *Denver Post* announced that the ambitious project would include not only the "greatest battles between soldiers and Indians" but Cody's service to the West from his boyhood to his career as a buffalo hunter, Indian scout, and "pacifier of the reds, greatest factor in the settlement of the plains, the real pathfinder and trail blazer, one to whom the West owes a debt of everlasting gratitude." The press pointed out the educational and entertainment value of seeing the real Buffalo Bill and many of the "self-same Indians who aimed the deadly arrows at his waving locks."[20]

Cody returned to Wyoming in the company of Essanay photographer and cameraman Charles Kaufman. At the time they were setting the film's groundwork, Prince Albert of Monaco was on his way to Wyoming for a previously planned hunt with Cody and sportsman A. A. Anderson. The prestigious visit to America was the first of a reigning European monarch. Albert's timing was rather inconvenient for the filmmakers, but it nevertheless brought the town of Cody to national attention. A large crowd welcomed the prince with a parade on Sheridan Avenue, the main street, when on September 15 he arrived on the Burlington train.

When Cody arranged for the prince to meet and present a rifle to Plenty Coups, last chief of the Crow nation and long-time friend to whites, Kaufman captured the exchange on film. Title cards reveal the prince saying, "I wish to present you with this rifle to kill game only, not to fire against the white man, and hope you will keep it as long as you live." Plenty Coups, in town for the opening of the Park County Fair, reciprocated with a peace pipe, a beaded belt, and elk teeth, replying, "You are the ruler in a country across the Big Lake. I, too, am a ruler. My people once ruled this entire land. I thank you for your gift and ask you to accept this belt as token of remembrance." The hunt was to begin the next day, but Albert decided to stay over for the fair and presided over its opening.[21] During the fair, Kaufman recorded Indian dances, rodeo events, and a parade that included a "high-grade, up-to-date touring car, carrying Indians who sang war songs and played on their native instruments." Cody approved of the prince's participation in the moving pictures, thinking it "will add strength and value to the same."[22]

On the main street, where many old buildings including a hotel, saloon, and post office still stood, Kaufman set up his camera and filmed a western drama based on the town's founding days. He replaced current signs with crudely drawn replicas of the 1897 originals, renaming one old cabin "Hotel de Trego" and others the "Salune, Last Chance, Tom Purcell, Prop." and the "Cody Trading Company, Postoffice." Old-timers and current residents were cast in dramatic scenes. In one, hotel manager Mrs. Jake Schwoob welcomes a cowboy and cowgirl before Cody

Buffalo Bill and Prince Albert wait for Chief Plenty Coups in Cody, Wyo. (Buffalo Bill Museum and Grave, Lookout Mountain, Golden, Colo.)

and businessman George Beck drive up in a buggy. As the two men carry surveying instruments into the establishment, the bartender chucks a man into the street. Cody grabs the miscreant's arm to prevent him from pulling a gun before Sheriff Dahlman can arrest him.[23]

One bystander observed that "they are 'faking' typical scenes such as are generally supposed to characterize the 'wild and wooly.' Shooting up the town, saloon brawls, throwing the cowboys into the street, riding the ponies into the 'palaces.'. . . When the pictures are shown in the East and Europe the natives of those sections will have a weird idea of Wyoming."[24] Months later, when Cody first saw the footage, he wrote to Jake Schwoob, a longtime Cody store owner, to tell him that Mrs. Schwoob

A crowd gathers in front of the Hotel de Trego during a filmic reenactment of old Cody days. (Buffalo Bill Historical Center, Cody, Wyo., P.69.2049)

"shines" in the pictures. "Spoor," he said, "asked Wharton the Producer if she was a professional."[25]

Afterward, Cody led the hunting party into the Rocky Mountains. When they set up "Camp Monaco 1913" in one idyllic spot, Albert hoped to bag a bear, and Kaufman was there to record the event. As host, Cody did not hunt, but he helped out with chores, some of which Kaufman recorded, including a brief extant scene of him chopping firewood.[26] Cody later admitted it was "no pleasure job" to organize large hunting parties, but the publicity was worth it, particularly in terms of his incessant need for adulation. Shortly after the hunt, Cody wrote his attorney, "I am certainly in the lime light now if I ever was, and I will certainly keep it up because these moving pictures we are about to take will perpetuate me for future generations as well as for the present."[27]

Meanwhile, others involved in the upcoming war film were completing the details of their bailiwicks. Johnny Baker, comfortable with organizational tasks, was busy readying the cowboys, stagecoaches, prairie schooners, horses, Hotchkiss guns, and other equipment at Rushville, Nebraska, about twenty-five miles from Pine Ridge. General Miles, taking his role as technical advisor seriously, sent Baker a detailed list of fourteen recommendations for scenes he thought ought to be included. "It occurs to me that there should be a series of pictures representing the last general disaffection among the Indian tribes, the threatened uprising, the campaign and final surrender," he wrote. He suggested showing the Sioux "in their natural condition" engaged in hunting, councils, and religious exercises. The uprising would be next, with troops on the Indians' trail and Sitting Bull's death. Miles wanted to show the Indians and troops "in hostile array," the Indians' final surrender, the last review of the troops, and "the transformation of the Indians from war tribes to civilized, progressive, peaceful Indians." The finale ought to have portraits of prominent Indians and of the officers who achieved the permanent peace.[28]

In Denver, George Spoor, Essanay's commercial and general manager Charles F. Stark, and Vernon Day were also finalizing details. Back in Milwaukee, King completed the Warbonnet scenario and mailed it to Cody. In return, Tammen sent King a check with a note expressing his and Cody's satisfaction with the work and orders for the Summit Springs script.[29]

It was nearly time for "Camera" and "Action."

CHAPTER 7

On Location

*Just as the painted Indians . . . fight against the white man, so
did they fight before the motion picture camera.*

DENVER POST, OCT. 17, 1913

On October 2, 1913, Cody rode out of the hunting camp with
his son-in-law Fred Garlow, Prince Albert, and cameraman
Charles Kaufman. He had telegrams to answer and further preparations to attend to before setting out to meet the army officers
in Nebraska.[1]

As he was leaving Chicago, General Miles reiterated for
reporters, "They want me there to make sure that everything
that we do is historically correct. I shall take active part in it too,
perhaps. The idea is to give the whole thing from the start. . . .
They will fight again, but there will be no bullets. All that is
over." He felt confident "this will be one of the finest records in
the government archives."[2]

Theodore Wharton and Vernon Day, along with their wives,
and David Hargan had left Chicago on September 26 and were
already on the scene at Pine Ridge, going over Charles King's
scripts and plotting the lay of the land. As manager of the production, which would undoubtedly secure his reputation as a
"top notch producer," Wharton estimated costs would run about

$100,000. He described his position as being "hemmed in on one side by the U.S. Army and on the other by the Sioux Nation. I will have to fight my way out, or in other words, reproduce the last Indian Wars, historically correct. . . . We are using more than 1000 horses in the production, and this is not a press agent's estimate either."[3] Considering the magnitude of the production, Wharton could have used not only his cameramen, but several assistant directors positioned around the area to deal with the multitude of unskilled, unprofessional actors. Instead, Wharton would have to rely heavily on Cody and Miles. In addition, he knew that prospective audiences were already aware of the denouement, so it remained to illustrate the events and Cody's role in them in the best light possible. The reenactment, enhanced by western topography, would emerge as a spectacle worthy of inclusion in any archives.

An outdoor film with action spread over a more extensive area than a studio required diligence on the part of the cameraman to keep scenes centered in the frame. By 1913, filmmakers were only occasionally using panning—sweeping the camera horizontally. The cameras Wharton brought may have been any of several models in use at the time. One, a lightweight Pathé model with a right-hand side crank, had a tendency to produce static in cold weather—generated when the celluloid film moved through the mechanism—making it potentially unreliable for the winter-like conditions expected on the South Dakota plains.[4] More likely, he carried the more expensive Bell & Howell cast aluminum camera, which Essanay was the first to use; after all, Donald Bell and Albert Howell were former Essanay employees. It had a tripod mount, a four-lens turret for close-up or wide-ranging scenes, and a variable-opening shutter. Some models had a speed indicator to keep the cameraman at an exact cranking speed of two turns per second. The crank continued to turn two or three times after release—exposing nearly two inches of film— but its "foolproof light trap" and ability to pan horizontally and

Men carry cameras on tripods onto the filming field at Pine Ridge. (Buffalo Bill Museum and Grave, Lookout Mountain, Golden, Colo.)

vertically made it ideal for scenes Wharton expected to film.[5] The film itself was contained in light-loading boxes (or magazines); three magazines, each carrying 400 feet of film, were sufficient for an average day's work.

Modern filmmakers might use dollies on tracks but, at the time, situating cameras on a moving vehicle was not yet a widely used technique. By 1915, when the renowned director D. W. Griffith mounted his camera on a truck to keep up with galloping horsemen, critics complained it was "an arty trick." Wharton did, however, mount his camera on a fifteen-foot wooden platform built onto a farm wagon and braced with ropes, the better to enjoy an unobstructed view of the landscape and action and to move the camera to various locations.[6]

En route from Wyoming, Cody and Wild West press agent John M. Burke spent a pleasant time at Fort Robinson near Crawford, Nebraska, consulting with Col. Horatio Sickel, whose Twelfth Cavalry's field infantry companies A, B, and D, were to play the soldiers of the 1890s Seventh Cavalry. Gen. Frank Baldwin and *Denver Post* correspondent Courtney Ryley Cooper joined them. The next day Cody met the train at Rushville, to which the Chicago & North Western hauled not only film equipment but also the other participating officers.

The troopers, four medical corpsmen, and a four-mule ambulance left Fort Robinson for the three-day march to the battlefield on Monday, October 6. Pvt. Harry Hollenbach found himself with a choice seat for the journey. After his commander ordered him to return with a comrade who had been horse-kicked, Hollenbach was stranded at Rushville. He met a civilian barber also headed to Wounded Knee and an army captain who agreed to corroborate that Hollenbach had not deserted. The officer told him Cody was at the hotel and would soon be leaving. On hearing his story, Cody invited Hollenbach to ride with him in his Packard touring car with Johnny Baker, John Burke, and some movie equipment. General Miles and the "movie mechanics" with their cameras, tripods, and film cases traveled in similar cars.[7]

Upon their arrival at Pine Ridge, General King scouted the Wounded Knee battlefield, spoke to survivor Joe Horn Cloud, and discussed the situation with other officers and agency personnel. He concluded, despite the company's extensive preparations, that a reenactment should not be filmed. As much as Cody respected the general, the battle was to be the highlight of the movie, and he planned to proceed. He did, however, promise King he would withhold the film from general viewing until the War Department approved its release.[8]

The Indians also arrived from miles around, some in wagons, others on horseback. Mrs. Cody, who accompanied her husband, recalled the Indians' delight at seeing him again. Many were old hands at filmmaking, having participated in the Miller Brothers show and Thomas Ince's westerns. Short Bull, who had visited Wovoka "and is blamed (unjustly, he declares) for the war," along with No Neck, Woman's Dress, Old Flat Iron, and other elders, came with their sons and sons of those who had died in the original battle. They warmly greeted the generals, particularly Miles, whom they called "Bear Coat" for the fur coat he often wore.[9]

Compelled to remain inside during a heavy snowstorm but comfortable thanks to oil heaters, Mrs. Vernon Day wrote to a friend that she found the Indians a "queer race of people but crafty & scheming." Outside, the racket from someone banging on a tomtom pervaded the area where nearly 375 tipis surrounded the Day tent. The thumping sound, reported Ryley Cooper, brought happiness to the Sioux, "sending 1913 into the days of the far past."[10]

Despite temperatures so cold that water froze in pails, Indian women began building a village of tipis covering acres along the creek. The script called for a fire to destroy them and other

Johnny Baker, Mrs. Vernon Day, Short Bull, wife of Short Bull, and Vernon Day pose for the camera. (Buffalo Bill Museum and Grave, Lookout Mountain, Golden, Colo.)

hastily constructed buildings. In another area, a wagon train was growing that also would burn "in strict accordance with history." Extensive building of sets only to have them destroyed added greatly to the expenses; one contemporary filmmaker had spent $1,500 (nearly $35,000 in 2010 dollars) building a replica of a Western border town.[11]

The biographer Richard Walsh mentions the Indians enjoying a merry-go-round that Cody hired to compensate them for their labor involved in preparing the sets. Hollenbach recalled Annie Oakley's surprise visit and exhibition of glass ball shooting.[12] However, biographies of Oakley place her elsewhere at this time; other sources surmise that Johnny Baker gave the marksmanship demonstration.

The soldiers pitched camp about eighteen miles from the agency. Soon the producers, including Baker, met with them to deliver instructions and to issue 1890-era accoutrements and weapons as well as blue army overcoats to replace their khaki-colored uniforms. In the interest of safety, Baker withheld ammunition, even blanks, from everyone until just before it was needed.[13]

As expected, the appearance of soldiers armed with Hotchkiss guns and rifles agitated the Sioux, who were sure they were about to be annihilated by the Twelfth Cavalry as the Seventh had done to their ancestors. Those ignorant of film reenactments, but mindful of the original horrific massacre, wailed and sobbed. "I could hear them moan and holler at night," Hollenbach recalled. "We used blank ammunition but were afraid the Indians might do something. Finally, we had to put one in chains and put him in the stockade." Cody and Baker repeatedly explained that the film was for posterity, and that it offered the opportunity to set the record straight. It was "not to do them harm," but "old grudges, that long were forgotten, began to rise again."[14]

During rehearsals, Baker and Wharton told the enactors to act as they had done in the original battles. Only the leading characters had assigned places.[15] With professional actors, good results depended on staging a film much like staging a play, but directors and cameramen needed cooperation, adaptation, and compromise to get the most out of the nonprofessionals acting out Cody's script. In making his Indian films, director Thomas Ince had found that some Sioux resented participating in battle scenes in which they were defeated and had to be cajoled into playing the role of vanquished. To avert any harm befalling the white actors, he had padded their war clubs.[16] Wharton, too, almost found this tactic necessary.

Horn Cloud was only a youngster in 1890, but because several relatives had died in the original battle he wanted to play a chief. Baker explained that his age at the time precluded him from this role. Perturbed, Horn Cloud attempted to stop the filming by arguing that "it would disturb the spirits of his departed relatives and retard their progress in the happy hunting ground." He rode among the others, pleading for agreement. When Baker called the older chiefs together to determine their stance, they called Horn Cloud a "small head" and reiterated their cooperation with the film company. Afterward, watching the completed film, Baker noticed that "Horn Cloud seems to be one of the 'moving spirits,'" though he had not assumed any specific part.[17]

Pine Ridge superintendent John Brennan contacted Maj. James McLaughlin at Standing Rock agency to suggest that, since a large gathering of Indians would be present for the picture taking, McLaughlin might want to use the occasion to have a flag raising. During his expeditions for Rodman Wanamaker, Joseph Dixon had initiated such ceremonies to demonstrate Indian allegiance to the United States and to publicize Wanamaker's lobbying for Indian citizenship. McLaughlin agreed, and on October 9 the camp held an elaborate ceremony during which he handed out flags. The Indians swore allegiance after listening to a recorded message of peace from President Woodrow Wilson.[18]

Early on the morning of Saturday, October 11, the Indians received their guns and last-minute instructions. Rehearsals at the main camp, about a mile and a half south of the original site, included some variations on the 1890 battle "necessitated for prudential reasons," that is, in order to "avoid a deathly exactness." Then filming began in earnest with scenes of the army intercepting Big Foot's band at Porcupine Butte, their escort to Wounded Knee, and the soldiers demanding the surrender of Indian arms. All that day the "man on the tower" caught every move "with his large revolving camera." Philip Wells, former scout and interpreter who had participated in the original battle, hurried around the scene, since he "knew better than any one just how things were and should be arranged." Col. James W.

Forsyth, the Seventh Cavalry commander in 1890 who had also taken part in the battle, offered suggestions. To film the event, Wharton required two days and used 13,000 feet of negatives.[19]

One evening, when the men were sitting around a campfire, Wells explained the origin of the name Wounded Knee. During a time when the Sioux and Crow tribes were fighting, one brave Sioux warrior had led his people to multiple victories until the day an enemy arrow struck his knee. When neither he nor the others could pull it out, blood poisoning spread throughout his body. His friends fought beside him until he died, then buried him near the creek where he fell and called it "Creek Where the Man with the Wounded Knee Was Buried."[20]

Chief Woman's Dress added wood to the blaze and bragged that he had saved Gen. George Crook by warning of Crazy Horse's plot to kill him. Paint still smeared the chief's face from the day's reenactment, and someone asked Wells if the paint was symbolic. His understanding was that there really was no such thing as war paint. Indians paint their faces black to mourn someone, Wells believed, but generally they would paint themselves for dancing as well as for battle.[21]

During the campfire talks, reporter Ryley Cooper heard debates about the government keeping, or flouting, Indian treaties. In this camp, "filled with aged redmen wise in Indian lore, noted generals and scouts with records in frontier history, agents and friends, all memories (up to a few last years) fail to bring forth the date and location of 'a square deal.'" Instead, Cooper found the officers expressing admiration and sympathy for the Indians' suffering in the face of the severe reprisals the army exacted.[22]

Sometimes humor characterized the conversation. Cody's friend Mike Russell revealed that he came west hoping for Indian adventures but was cured of the yearning when he came upon corpses of eight people killed by Indians. General Baldwin related the story of being bayoneted by a soldier. Knowing that cold can bring on drowsiness, he had ordered his soldiers to bayonet a fellow caught sleeping, not guessing he would be the object of such a stimulating wake-up. In his turn, General Lee invented a tale about three men who went up a hill and no one ever saw them again. "Good Lord," exclaimed Cody," What became of them?" "Went down the other side," replied Lee.[23]

The frivolity ended on October 13, when Wharton's timetable called for the reenactment of the Wounded Knee battle. The previous evening, Chief Iron Tail heard that some younger Indians resolved to avenge the deaths of their forefathers by using real bullets instead of blanks. Short Bull and others who had traveled with Cody's Wild West knew the futility of such action; they had seen the retaliation white men could perpetrate. They advised Cody of the situation, and he called a council. Finally, reason prevailed, and no second battle of Wounded Knee occurred. Some historians doubt the story's veracity, claiming it was a rumor Cody hyped to enhance its effect as a promotional gimmick.[24]

One legitimate motive for such a Sioux reaction was Miles's insistence that the battle be reenacted exactly where the massacre had occurred, in this instance over the victims' graves. After missionaries taught them Christianity and other white beliefs, Sioux rarely followed the tradition of laying out their dead on scaffolds or in trees. But in 1890, adding further insult, the military had hired civilians to gather the frozen corpses into wagons and dump them into mass graves. Miles's removal of the grave markers was tantamount to further disrespect and tactlessness.

Inconsistent with his insistence on accuracy, Miles protested Cody's plan to film all the grisly details including the massacre of women and children. As commander of the campaign, Miles believed the massacre could have been avoided and thought reenacting the butchery countermanded the Indians' welfare. Therefore, he refused to take part, talked Superintendent Brennan into disallowing the more brutal aspects, and remained at the

Cody on location at Pine Ridge. (Buffalo Bill Museum and Grave, Lookout Mountain, Golden, Colo.)

agency during the reenactment. Reporting Miles's objections, Cooper wrote to *Denver Post* managing editor E. C. Shepard, "If any of my stuff speaks of the general in connection with the battle, please cut it out. Gen. Miles objects to headlines or any references to himself in connection with the battle. . . . None of the generals were present at Wounded Knee and object to being coupled with it." Cody told another reporter that "no amount of money" could tempt Miles to be present.[25]

Because the Wounded Knee battle was the mainstay of the production, Wharton employed "scene dissection" during the taking of the scenes—using three cameras in sundry positions—and planned to knit the shots together during editing. The result would provide a greater illusion of reality in the finished product. In complex spectacles such as this, with expansive sets, huge crowds, and enormous sweep of action, the benefit was a diversity viewers normally found only in shorter studio films.[26]

The military men had prepared Wharton with an overview of the original battle: On December 29, 1890, Forsyth's Seventh Cavalry surrounded Chief Big Foot's band of 350 Indians. The troopers were to disarm them and lead them to Pine Ridge. As Forsyth and a pneumonia-suffering Big Foot parleyed, a medicine man, Yellow Bird (or Sits Up Straight), began to dance and throw dust into the air, urging the Sioux not to give up the Ghost Dance tenets, for then the soldiers' bullets would float away like dust.

Philip Wells detected in the medicine man's intonations an ominous note that presaged no good. Instead of the Indians acquiescing peacefully, they stalled, unsure what to do. Irritated with their reluctance, Forsyth ordered each one searched. Wise elders submitted, but younger warriors brandished their rifles, and someone—possibly a deaf Indian who had not heard the order—fired on the already tense soldiers. The camp exploded with gunfire from both sides. Indians fled into the ravine as the army's hilltop artillery lobbed shells into their midst.

Survivors reported seeing soldiers and Indians in hand-to-hand combat. Horrific reports—of Capt. George Wallace's head being bashed in, of Big Foot's daughter rushing to her father's side only to be executed there, of enraged soldiers shooting into Indian corpses, of dead Indian women curled around the bodies of their dead children, of a young boy deliberately shot in both hips—were told and transcribed at the official investigation.[27] One warrior attacked a Catholic priest, Father Francis Craft, with a sharp knife. When Wells came to his defense to deflect the blow, the same Indian nearly cut off his nose before Wells could shoot his assailant. As the battle raged, Wells held onto his bloody nose until army surgeon C. B. Ewing could sew it back on. When the acrid smoke cleared and all was silent on the snowy day except for the screams and moans of the wounded and dying, Big Foot sprawled dead on the ground with nearly two hundred of his people.[28]

Twenty-three years later, Mrs. Brennan, wife of the agency's superintendent, watched as Wharton, through interpreters Joe Horn Cloud, Ben American Horse, Jacob White Eyes, and Jim Grass, explained what he wanted the Indians to do. The reenactment was to be so exact that he required hours of rehearsal. Wells entered the "circle of death" as he had so long ago. Twice the participants practiced the part "where the Indian threw the dust." War-painted and feathered, Short Bull pointed his rifle at the soldiers "with the aim of old," and Lone Bear readied to play the part of Big Foot.[29] It is not known if Wharton had the reenactors speak their parts or merely move their lips to indicate speech. Large pantomime movements conveyed all the emotions, and intertitles inserted between frames during post-production would suggest actual dialogue. Mrs. Brennan wrote her daughter, "You would never believe Indians would act like they did. They entered into it and did so fine everybody was surprised."[30]

Watching the rehearsals along with Cody, Baldwin, and Mike Russell were thousands of people who came from all over the reservation and nearby towns. Ryley Cooper estimated that more than five hundred automobiles arrived loaded with spectators. During the reenactment, "they did not speak—but they leaned forward, their hands clasped tight, their lips drawn in a thin line of excitement, their eyes aflash with the thrill of it all."[31]

When cameras ceased rolling on the reenactment of the bloody business, Cody made much of the fact that some Indians had been too excited to remain "dead" and rolled over to watch the others "die." "Thus," he remembered, "comedy is injected into an otherwise very serious affair." Unfortunately, his version of amused Indians contradicts his story of scheming Indians intent on revenge. He boasted the next day, "If all the pictures are as true to detail as this . . . there will be no approaching them for quality."[32] As a result of Brennan siding with Miles, no women or children participated, notwithstanding the fact that in 1890 soldiers had killed them with as much abandon as the men. Despite his deep regard for the Indians, this may have rankled Cody; he and Ryley Cooper had repeatedly promoted the film's historical accuracy.

The next day, Indians and soldiers broke camp and headed to Pine Ridge four miles away on White Clay Creek to film the battle of Holy Rosary Mission, also known as Drexel Mission. Miles and Wharton walked the grounds and conversed about the events that had occurred there.

In 1890, the day after the Wounded Knee battle, other Ghost Dancers had fled after hearing news of the massacre. On the way, they burned several log buildings at the mission. One trooper died and six others were wounded when Sioux ambushed a Seventh Cavalry squadron responding to the fires along with a relief force from the Ninth Cavalry, which together with the Tenth were known as "Buffalo Soldiers," under the command of Gen. Guy Henry. Miles, fearing a full-blown assault, had sent a courier to the Indians asking for a peaceful resolution. "We want no treaty; we are here to fight," they retorted.[33] But, with the multitude of troopers, resistance was futile. Miles urged their surrender and promised fair treatment, all the while circling his troops closer. The Indians argued among themselves over whether they could trust him until they eventually had no choice. Last to surrender was Dewey Beard, who appeared in the film in his original ghost shirt with its five bullet holes. With the troopers' backing, Miles's diplomacy had averted a tragedy potentially greater than Wounded Knee.[34]

Cody and Miles debated filming the mission battle and decided for it. Indians and soldiers in blue battled the freezing elements and each other. Short Bull and Kicking Bear "raised their cry which sent the hostiles flooding to the bad lands; it took them back to days of sorry and of worry." Miles rode back and forth

Theodore Wharton and Gen. Nelson Miles walk the battlefield.
(Buffalo Bill Museum and Grave, Lookout Mountain, Golden, Colo.)

in front of them directing. For *Post* readers, Cooper compared the mission battle with Wounded Knee. At the latter, "the white man was the aggressor. They outnumbered the Indians. The red men were crowded into a ravine where lines of bullets sent them to death." But at the mission, "the Indian was the aggressor and he fought in his own style. There his pony circled and swung. There he sang to the cutting wind, there his rifle cracked with far greater effect than at Wounded Knee." During filming, the people sang the ghost songs again and, "as the wailing cry mounted, higher and higher, as the sobs came, one by one the warriors stalked forward to lay their heads upon the shoulder of some weeping Indian woman, then stalk on again. Again there were tears and the clasping of hands, for memory and grief can live long in the heart of an Indian."[35]

Cooper was impressed with the scenes at the mission and guessed they outclassed those taken at Wounded Knee. Reliving the past was grueling for many Indians, but some had let the memories go. He related the story of Chief Thick Bread, "whittling at a great wooden knife, waiting for the time when he was to sally forth with his band, to reproduce the historic fights" and singing as he worked. At the sight of a bald visitor, Bread pretended to scalp him and then produced a shank of hair he claimed he had taken from Pawnee chief Omaha.[36]

The next scenes involved the councils Miles and his staff had held with the Indians, the review of the troops on agency parade grounds, and the delivery of hostages. Miles, who in 1890 had moved his command to the scene, watched in 1913 with the army and its wagons on one side of the square as scout Wells led the hostages forward with Short Bull in front. The Indians were dressed "in their great bonnets and masses of bead work. . . . Beautiful eagle feathers swayed in the wind, tobacco bags, wonderful in their workings, dangled from the wrists of the red men as they came forward." Several sources contend that Miles demanded cavalrymen march past the cameras until it appeared

Gen. Jesse Lee leads the Brulés to the agency. (Buffalo Bill Museum and Grave, Lookout Mountain, Golden, Colo.)

that all 11,000 men in his original command had been filmed. His purpose in 1891 was to show the Indians the force of the U.S. Army in order to dissuade them from further rebellion. It is easy to imagine Cody and Wharton grinding their teeth at the delay and expense, but theirs was the last laugh when, though the cameraman continued cranking for effect, the film ran out.[37]

Before soldiers and Indians left to film the Badlands scenes, Wharton completed those of the hostile Brulés' removal to the Rosebud agency and the other Indians' break for the Badlands stronghold. On Monday, October 20, remarkable for its "clear atmosphere [which] adds wonderfully to the quality and tone of the pictures," Gen. Jesse Lee led the reproduction of the January 1891 removal.[38]

The next day, October 21, the motion picture camp split up. One unit remained at Pine Ridge, the other with generals Baldwin and Miles headed out. To show the conditions the soldiers had to endure throughout the campaign, Miles insisted once again that those scenes take place exactly where the original had occurred—about fifty miles north of Pine Ridge—even though only one narrow wagon road accessed the exceptionally rough terrain. Snowstorms were common in that season and, even if they made good time going in, it was doubtful the exit would be easy. Cody, willing to sacrifice reality for expediency, argued that the trip would add time and expense to the project and was willing to use a similar-looking proximate location, but Miles was adamant. During his career, he gave orders expecting they would be carried out, and he did not take kindly to Cody's insubordination. The resulting antagonism between the two friends never completely healed, though Cody's point was proved when inclement weather delayed the foray for a day.[39]

Cooper justly credited Baker as "a power in the taking of pictures." Diplomatically, Baker stepped between Miles and Cody and maintained that he would "take the Indians and troops in there and I'll bring them out again. . . . And there will be pictures in the cameras when they come out." He started with twenty-five wagons and rations for eight days. Miles and Baldwin followed the next day after participating in the filming of a sort of who's who of characters.[40]

The Indians' hideout lay in a valley nearly inaccessible to horses until a trail was found along the rim of the basin. Miles called the stronghold the "Gibraltar of the Indians" and said, "the Pass of Thermopylae lessens in strategic importance by the side of the Bad Lands." After the soldiers and Indians managed to lower tents and provisions with ropes, even Miles camped on-site in a tent.[41]

When the required scenes were on film, soldiers pulled their comrades up the steep precipice and started back. The first day's travel went well, but the next day a blizzard struck. With only two days' rations left, the cavalry led the return. Cameramen took shots of them traipsing through the snow just as the soldiers had done in 1890. His mission accomplished, Miles headed for home. Baldwin returned to Pine Ridge before leaving for Denver.[42]

When a cold dark day prevented the filming of Sitting Bull's death and Short Bull's journey to meet the messiah Wovoka, Wharton focused on scenes showing the Indians' progress. "A busy day at the agency, farming scenes on the Indians' lands, the marketing of their products, children in the agency schools studying books and learning trades, the fine horses and cattle on allotted lands, dairying" proved how the Indians had become civilized. A seven-passenger touring car—"the last word in civilization"—also made it onto the film.[43]

On October 28, Wharton finally completed the Wounded Knee segments. Cody was delighted and predicted that "the pictures will be a great success. . . . The Indians all worked well, the soldiers did excellent work and the hearts of everyone were in their tasks."[44] The next day, Cody and Wharton, along with the soldiers and Indians, worked at getting the Summit Springs and Warbonnet battles filmed according to King's scenarios. Lt. Ralph Talbot took King's role in the Warbonnet scenes. The officer who had chosen Talbot later told King he selected soldier-actors "who would in part, at least, portray the dash and vitality which had been shown by the actors in the real scenes years before." When King saw "himself" on screen, he remarked that Talbot "did the thing better than I could."[45]

Nearly 30,000 feet of film filled Essanay cameras and contained pictures of almost three thousand men, women, and horses in action extending over miles. Before the company prepared to leave for home, everyone celebrated with a feast. Because Wharton had impressed the Sioux with his "courteous rule" over them, they pronounced him honorary chief Wambli Wicasa (Eagle Man). Mrs. Vernon Day earned an Indian name meaning "good Ogallala woman" for her kindness and was adopted as a tribal daughter. Day paid $1,313.48 to fifty-three Indians who were with the Wild West show at its dissolution but had not received their pay.[46] By rights, half the payment should have come from Lillie, but Cody told them, "I want all you boys to be satisfied. . . . I don't want one of you to suffer and I am not going to allow it. You need the money and you are going to have it. You have been my friends and I am going to be yours." The film company paid the other Indians $1.50 per day as well as hay and grain for their horses.[47]

The soldiers returned to Fort Robinson. Later that fall, they headed to the Navajo reservation in New Mexico to enforce orders of the Indian agent. The trouble was resolved shortly, and they boasted of their accomplishments. "Nothing can harm us. We've all been killed from five to seven times each in the bloody war campaign against the Sioux which we have just finished in splendid style . . . up at Pine Ridge." "And Indians," continued the first squadron's commander, "why, we eat 'em up. True, I was hit over the head with a war club in the battle of Wounded Knee and I reluctantly deceased. But that was in fair fight and the Indian was welcome to his laurels. But we won all the battles and concluded the campaign gloriously."[48]

Doubtless, Cody was glad the "remarkable, exciting hard working trip" was completed. After coping with Miles's insistence on his way, the inclement weather, and the Indians' grief, he considered filmmaking, even of the "greatest motion pictures ever taken," harder than "three circuses in one."[49] Back in Wyoming, after all the preparations and weeks of hard work, he and old friend John Reckless Davis left on a hunt accompanied only by a cook and a horse wrangler. Last to leave were cameraman David Hargan and Vernon Day. On their way home, Mr. and Mrs. Wharton visited Fort Robinson, where he shot 800 feet of negatives showing the regiment's skill in "horsemanship and daring."[50]

CHAPTER 8

Post-Production

We finally understood that the cinema was not a perfected toy but the terrible and magnificent flag of life.
PHILLIPPE SOUPAULT, "CINEMA U.S.A" (1924)

Unlike many film manufacturers, Essanay, to save the expense of making positive prints, compelled its directors to edit from negatives.[1] Thus, Theodore Wharton worked for two months compiling those he brought back to the Chicago plant from Pine Ridge. After first removing the films from their sealed tin cases, technicians wound them on wooden racks in a dust-free darkroom, then placed them in a developer for a precise length of time. The film was dried and polished by women using chemical solutions developed especially for that purpose. Because he filmed out of historical sequence, Wharton had numbered each scene and kept a record of the footage. At the time, the average film reel contained 1,000 feet of film, or 16,000 frames, perhaps half of which would end up cut or needing to be refilmed. Even professional cameramen managed to get good pictures only a third of the time, so during the assembly of the various lengths of film Wharton removed those where the light was bad, where static had caused streaks, or where the focus was unclear.[2] For scenes in which more than one camera had captured the action,

Wharton organized the fragments into a smooth continuum, critiquing them for length and placement of intertitles.

The negatives were then run through a printing machine to make positive stock and perforated. The final layout was projected onto a screen so that other directors could offer suggestions or criticisms. When the film was approved, assemblers used it as a standard from which to make duplicates. His assignment accomplished, shortly thereafter Wharton resigned and left for Ithaca, New York, where he and his brother Leopold formed their own company, eventually becoming the city's most famous silent film producers.[3]

At the beginning of the filming, Ryley Cooper had sent a copy of Wharton's scenarios to the *Denver Post*. The brief phrases describe the film's "motion tableaux" and reflect the serial nature of the film.[4] Wharton did not have to follow his proposed sequences to the letter but could vary the action as his experience and the situation dictated, still keeping to historical accuracy as the project demanded. Since only a three-minute fragment and a series of still photographs remain today, the list is important for providing one clue to what *The Indian Wars* film contained:[5]

First—Indians in their natural condition, showing Indian life, habitations, occupation, devotion, amusements, sports, etc.

Second—Distressed condition of Indians, great poverty, causing disaffection and hostility.

Third—Receiving intelligence of the return of the Messiah to the earth, and the starting of emissaries to see him in response to his summons.

Fourth—Their journey toward the setting sun to meet the so-called Redeemer.

Fifth—Received with great solemnity by the Messiah. His revelations, prophecy, and admonitions.

Sixth—Return of the emissaries and consternation in the Indian camps. Demonstrations of great joy and thanksgiving.

Seventh—Great war council. War dances. Hostile demonstrations.

Eighth—Rush of the Indian tribes to the bad lands. Hostile demonstrations.

Ninth—Occupation and hostile demonstrations in their strongholds in the Mauvassas or Bad Lands.

Tenth—Charge of mounted Indians.

Eleventh—Cavalry charge.

Twelfth—Arrest and death of Sitting Bull.

Thirteenth—Troops in order of battle.

Fourteenth—Surrender of Hump and his warriors to Capt. Ewers.

Fifteenth—Council between the division commander and the Indian chiefs.

Sixteenth—Movement of a large camp of Indians toward the agency to surrender.

Seventeenth—Engagement at Wounded Knee.

Eighteenth—Engagement on White Clay Creek near Mission.

Nineteenth—Final surrender of the Indians and close of the Indian wars.

Twentieth—Officers viewing large hostile camp.

Twenty-first—Final review of the troops before their dispersement.

Twenty-second—Surrender of leaders of the hostile Indians as hostages for the permanent peace of the Indian tribe.

Twenty-third—Return of hostile Brulés under Captain Lee.

Twenty-fourth—Return of hostile Cheyennes under Captain Ewers.

Twenty-fifth—Indians in peaceful condition of industry and prosperity.

Twenty-sixth—Portraits of prominent Indians.

Twenty-seventh—Portraits of men who were distinguished in Indian wars and rendered important service in securing permanent peace.

The press later reported that Essanay might include the flag-raising scenes. No recording remains of music played during the showings, though one reviewer spoke of hearing the bugle, national airs, and Indian music.[6] "Speaking pictures" were still undergoing trials to overcome problems with synchronization, amplification, and fidelity, but sound effects supplied by various firms were widely used at the time. Cries of the wounded, running horses, Hotchkiss guns, and officers barking commands doubt-less intensified the already powerful film, but "talkies" them-selves remained a novelty outside the realm of Cody's film.[7]

Buffalo Bill and Harry Tammen were in Chicago the last week of December for their first view of the assembled pictures. Cody's initial impression was that "the pictures are great but a little close up dramatic. Knock out stunts will better them immensely." With him were Colonel Schunk and Agent McLaughlin. After seeing the film, they asked to be a part of it. Essanay agreed and extra pictures were taken.[8]

Cody was eager to get the films out to the public, anticipating "all kinds of money" flowing in. Several American exhibitors had already offered him "big money," but Spoor advised him not to get anxious, to consider the offers he had received from Europe as well. He also recommended they send the film out to fifteen or twenty exhibitors and show it first in high-priced theaters, "then the 5 & 10 houses."[9]

Meanwhile, in Milwaukee, General King grew chagrined at the unfavorable publicity he received as a result of his connec-tion with the film. The press included him among the officers they assumed had been "charging and recharging [Indians] while the cameras clicked." As a proud and professional officer, King asked John G. Gregory, fellow member of the Milwaukee Press Club, to help quell curious questions about when he would again appear as an "Indian-killer." King personally wrote to the *Evening Wisconsin* editor that "no one of the Generals named [in the *Wisconsin*'s provocative article and in the *Chicago Tribune*'s similar piece], nor Cody himself, took any part whatever in that midwinter and most unfortunate battle. No one of them took any part in the photographic representation of its reproduction." Especially irritating was the assumption that the men went only to have themselves photographed fighting fake battles.[10] The *Army and Navy Journal* took up his defense, quoting King insisting that General Miles and the others returned to Pine Ridge to film the great peace congress, not a battle. After all, the Indians had great respect for Miles, "the big chief who showed them the right road."[11]

On January 10, 1914, Cody arrived in Lawton, Oklahoma, with another Essanay producer—Mr. Horton—to film additional scenes at Fort Sill. With Fifth Field Artillery soldiers and nearby Comanches, Cody hoped to capture additional scenes of contemporary Indian schools, farms, and houses. Johnny Baker assisted with the script writing, probably with suggestions from Frank Baldwin, the fort's first Indian agent. In spite of its alleged purpose of demonstrating postwar peaceful situations, the script called for a scene similar to that of the Summit Springs battle showing the Indians' more savage nature: They capture two white women and Cody is prevailed on to help. He sights the Indian camp and, determining that the cavalrymen are barely outnumbered, orders a charge. The "redskins," forced to fight in the open, take flight. Cody rushes for the chief's tent, where he expects to find the captured women, played by Mrs. Theodore Wharton and her friend Mrs. Olive Word Titterington, but he arrives too late. Mrs. Titterington has already been "slain" and Mrs. Wharton "severely wounded by the tomahawk."[12]

A week later at the First National Bank building of Chicago, Cody held a private showing for the film's military advisors and financial backers. Besides Tammen, among those present were generals Miles, Wheaton, Stewart, King, and Baldwin; colonels Schunk, Baker, Kingsbury, McCarthy, Kimball, McDonald; Major Ray; Captain Billingsley; and Cy de Vry, H. H. Cross, W. L. Parks,

Cody reenacts the rescue of the women hostages at Summit Springs.
(Buffalo Bill Historical Center, Cody, Wyo., P.69.2065)

Milward Adams, Frederic Bonfils, and Lou Housemann.[13] The
first reel opened with an introduction of the participants, including
many of those in the audience, as well as Short Bull ("Chief
Medicine Man and Messiah Craze Apostle"), scout Philip Wells,
and Chief Jack Red Cloud. They stand on a gray plain stretching
to the horizon. Snow flurries fill the air. After a bit, Chief Tall
Bull, "resplendent in beads and buckskins" rides into view.[14]

The film's program guide continues the story: in the "First
Battle Picture," the 1869 Summit Springs battle was fought against
Renegade Dog Soldiers who terrorized the settlers in Kansas,
Nebraska, and Colorado territories. From an attack on an emi-
grant train to glorious victory, army troops under command of
Eugene Carr and Cody trailed, located, and "worsted" the Indians
until finally "Tall Bull bit dust under Cody's knife."[15]

Following chronologically, the second reel focuses on the Battle of Warbonnet Creek from the 1876 campaign with officers Carr and Wesley Merritt; Cody again serves as chief of scouts. "Look, Lieutenant! There are the Indians!" proclaims an intertitle.

Along with the aged but still agile Cody, current Twelfth Cavalry commander Horatio Sickel squirms on his belly in the sagebrush—into a position he had taken decades previously as a young lieutenant—to watch a band of Cheyenne about to attack a wagon train. Again, title cards replace dialogue:

"The wagon train! But all that's wonderful; and we never thought they could make it."

"Get ready, Cody."

"Stay there, King! Watch till they're close to you. Then give the word."

Indians sight the soldiers and, seeing his old enemy Yellow Hair, Buffalo Bill on his horse Isham advances ahead of the troops, shouting a defiant challenge. The film captures the subsequent fight as he takes "the first scalp [in revenge] for Custer." Merritt and his troopers rout the rest of the Indians. General King, present during the original fight, directed the scene.

Reel no. 1 of the second section begins in spring 1890 when, learning of a messiah, the tribes send emissaries to hear the good news. The Indian playing Wovoka raises his arms to heaven as he instructs his apostles in the Ghost Dance. When Short Bull returns to his tribe, he tells his people to make and wear ghost shirts to protect themselves from soldiers' bullets. Sitting Bull, Kicking Bear, and other war chiefs become agitated, and the agent reports the Indians engaging in war dances. When commanders dispatch troops, frightened Indians flee to the Badlands.

Meanwhile, Miles asks Cody to induce Sitting Bull to come in to the agency, but President Harrison rescinds the order. Instead, the Indian police arrive to arrest the old chief. In a scene "of such action, suspense, desperate fighting that the palms of one's hands are wet and the lips dry," Sitting Bull attempts to go peacefully, but

Cody leads a company of soldiers across the Dakota plains. (Buffalo Bill Museum and Grave, Lookout Mountain, Golden, Colo.)

his son's taunts prompt him to call on his friends for aid. A subsequent fight portrays the death of Sitting Bull and six police.[16]

"Now we're coming to the battle of Wounded Knee," whispered Cody to his companions in the theater.

In reel no. 2—"The Rebellion"—Colonel Sumner and the Eighth Cavalry try to prevent Big Foot, reenacted by Lone Bear, and his band from entering the Badlands, but they escape and are intercepted by a regiment of the Seventh Cavalry under command of Maj. Samuel Whitside, played by one of the soldiers from Fort Robinson. Big Foot surrenders and, on learning that he is suffering from pneumonia, Whitside transfers him to an ambulance and begins the march back to Pine Ridge. They camp for the night on Wounded Knee Creek.

Reel no. 3 shows the events of December 29, 1890. Father Craft visits the camp, where the Indians offer him an eagle feather to show their goodwill. Colonel Forsyth arrives and, through interpreter Philip Wells, orders them to give up their guns; only a few comply. During a search for hidden weapons, someone shoots and a volley of gunfire ignites the battle. Through advance and retreat, soldiers drive the Indians into the ravine of Wounded Knee Creek. Lieutenant Sickel orders soldiers manning the Hotchkiss gun to sweep the area.

The army commanders in the audience leaned forward in their chairs, as intrigued as they were a quarter century previously. When the battle was over, General Miles "smiled severely." "They're historically correct," he said, "Just as they happened." Cody reportedly "chuckled" and said, "Seems like yesterday."[17]

Reel no. 4 shows the Ninth Cavalry arriving at Pine Ridge the next day after a hundred-mile march. With no time to rest, the tired troops send the Indians scattering throughout the hills. A blizzard rages, during which the original—and reenacting— soldiers wage the rest of the campaign. Finally, disheartened by successive defeats, Short Bull and Jack Red Cloud lead a delegation to council with General Miles. They agree to surrender and to deliver the most prominent chiefs as hostages. The on-screen Miles and his staff review the Indian camp as the real Miles sat, "silent and erect," watching himself. Colonel Schunk also saw himself, "intent and interested, skirmishing over the Badlands. Generals Stewart and Kingsbury [sat], eyes half closed, while the stirring scenes before them passed through their minds, more clearly perhaps than on the screen."[18]

The cinematic Indians are restless and fearful, but Capt. (now a general) Jesse Lee arrives with John Burke to reassure them on reel no. 5. Lee promises to escort them personally to their homes. Tableaux show Lee befriending the Brulés, and Burke the Ogallalas. Afterward, Miles receives their oath of allegiance. A review of "victorious troops in a biting snowstorm, bands playing, guidons fluttering, flags waving and the final exit of twenty-seven chiefs who give themselves as hostage to the nation" follows.[19]

The final reel, "School Days and Now—1914," depicts Market Holiday at Pine Ridge, modern buildings, and children in school uniforms playing in a brass band. "Thus ends the transition of the Red Man from Warpath to Peace Pursuits under the American Flag—'The Star Spangled Banner.' Finis."

When the lights came up, many in the audience sat awestruck. The film was not escapism or fantasy, and the aftereffects were difficult for the military men in a heightened state of suggestibility to contend with. The emotional film intimated far more than a mere movie. It was truly life and death. Brigadier General Hall, a veteran of the 1876 campaign, turned to Cody. "Bill, I didn't think it could be done. . . . I didn't think until I saw these pictures that it would be possible to reproduce what we went through out there."[20]

Despite having had a good deal of input into the production, three days after the viewing General Miles wrote a long impassioned letter to Essanay's George Spoor protesting "the misrepresentation and misleading statements made in regard to those pictures." Citing the oft-claimed authenticity, Miles was aggrieved that the project had been filmed out of sequence and in October, not midwinter. Also, the council between Lee, Burke, and the Indians happened several days after the surrender, not before the close of the campaign. Miles also said it simply was not true that the Sioux were promised they would not be punished if they surrendered. He complained about the intertitle introducing the "War of the Messiah," arguing its ambiguity— that it might stand for "some of the Roman wars or Crusades." Cody's name appeared above and below the intertitle "The Close of the Indian Wars in America" as though they were "manouevered at the dictation of Colonel Cody." Still smarting from his rows with the showman during filming, Miles petulantly argued, "If it is the object of the enterprise to exploit the events in the life of William Cody I have nothing to say," but if a historical presentation was the purpose, then, as an officer, he objected to the way the troops were used. He complimented Essanay's artists as "skillful men . . . anxious to do good work;" however, he wanted his name and any scene with him in it removed.[21] Then, hoping to enlist Frank Baldwin's support, Miles wrote him that "this fraud and outrage of the army ought not to be encouraged or permitted. Cody always has represented the soldiers and citizens secondary and insignificant to the 'Cow Boys.'"[22]

Cody learned of Miles's disapproval and also wrote to Baldwin acknowledging Miles's reproach. He had all the pictures and titles changed as Miles requested, though the situation "much distressed" him. Heading back to Wyoming, Cody asked Baldwin to tell Miles that "knowing me as he does that I never placed myself where I was not entitled to be."[23]

Meanwhile, Charles King returned to Chicago to help edit additional segments of the Warbonnet reel. One part showed Cody shooting and scalping Yellow Hair, but King was now hedging that the scalping had ever taken place in the original battle. Cody had replayed the scene so many times onstage that he had come to believe it happened that way, and King, in the interests of accuracy, wanted no part of the fantasy. He told the Chicago press, "It is true that I have been helping in the scenario and staging of these pictures, for at War Bonnet at least, Cody and I were close together and I saw the start of his duel with Yellow Hand, but not the finish, as I was rather busy myself at the time. But when the papers describe me as 'reenacting on the field' the somewhat active part demanded of me some forty years ago, they are far too flattering."[24]

Cody spent ten days in Wyoming and at his TE Ranch preparing a lecture to accompany the film. After 1908 many exhibitors featured a speaker, sometimes the film's star, who explained ambiguous points in the action between reels when documentaries, and even story films, grew more complex. Audiences easily understood short films, but multireelers like *The Indian Wars* required supplementary clarification.[25]

He enlisted his son-in-law Fred Garlow to tour with the film throughout Nebraska and also signed with Motograph Company to handle the earlier Wild West pictures.[26] Cody then left for Washington, where he had scheduled a private matinee of the film, now titled *The Last Indian Battles, or From the Warpath to the Peace Pipe*, at the Home Club of the Interior Department on Thursday, February 26, his sixty-eighth birthday. Attendees included the director of the Bureau of Mines, Commissioner Ewing of the Patent Office, and Mrs. Eugene Carr, widow of the general.[27] Before the film began, Wyoming senator Francis E. Warren touted Cody as "one of my constituents, and while a young man, he probably is the oldest and most distinguished of the pioneers in America—if not in the world." Cody, "still straight as the arrows that have whizzed around his noble head on many a hard-fought battle-field," told the audience his desire "to preserve history by the aid of the camera, with the living participants who took an active part in the closing Indian wars of America."[28]

Such a project had never been attempted. Because many of the original participants had grown too old or died, the films were already valuable since the events could not be reproduced again.

The evening presentation at the Columbia Theater was the most crucial. Formal invitations to the event had gone out to President Woodrow Wilson (who was unable to attend), Secretary and Mrs. Lane, Secretary of Labor William Wilson, Secretary Garrison, Commissioner of Indian Affairs Cato Sells, Commissioner of General Land Office Clay Tallman, and an assortment of senators, representatives, and cabinet members. Secretary Lane introduced Cody to the assembly as the man "whose enterprise and genius have given to future generations vivid historical pictures of great events in the conquest of the West." In his remarks, Cody explained: "If these pictures lack anything in dramatic effect it is because they have been taken true to life with no attempt to stage the production, as in actual war there is no time or purpose to pose for the camera." He described each of the battles on the six miles of film. Relating his dispatching of Yellow Hair "to the happy hunting grounds from which he never returned to say what he found there" and the battle "where soldiers dripped with Indians' blood and Indians washed their hands in soldiers' gore," Cody held the audience enthralled. He could not resist boasting: "Having been an actor in those early wars, having played my part with all the courage that was in me, courage kept warm and burning by my love for my country and my hope of a better day when all men shall stand as brothers under a common flag, I know that the pictures you look upon tonight are true to life."[29] Program text, styled in John Burke's typical ostentatious prose, noted the film's purpose to "arouse patriotic sentiment and show the untraveled that the Peace Congress leaves them a legacy to preserve—the freedom of the white-winged Angel of Peace to fly untrammeled from ocean to ocean and warble the hymn of Amity to the world."[30]

First Public Presentation

AT THE

COLUMBIA THEATRE

WASHINGTON, D. C.

COL. W. F. CODY
(Buffalo Bill)
As He is Today

February 27
1914

**UNDER AUSPICES
OF THE**

National Press Club.

THE COL. W. F. CODY

(Buffalo Bill)

Historical Pictures Company

DEPICTING THE

LAST INDIAN BATTLES

AND FINAL SURRENDER TO

Lieutenant-General Nelson A. Miles

WITH

COLONEL W. F. CODY--BUFFALO BILL

as Chief of Scouts, under whose Personal
Directions these Historical Moving
Pictures Were Produced by the

ESSANAY FILM MANUFACTURING COMPANY, of CHICAGO, ILL.

Dignitaries who attended *The Indian Wars'* first public showing received a program detailing its history. (Buffalo Bill Historical Center, Association files, Buffalo Bill Museum, Curator's office, Cody, Wyo.)

The next day, the *Washington Herald* raved over the beautiful and inspiring scenes that "impress through the terrible realism they show."[31] As he had filled his Wild West show program guides with commendations and letters of praise from prominent generals and heads of state, Cody, seeking promotional endorsement for the film, asked General Baldwin for a letter "with an expression of your views on the subject and your opinion as to the value of these films for historic and educational purposes."[32] Baldwin replied with a quotable quote:

> I with the public have been able to witness the reproduction by film moving picture process many of the scenes of the last Indian wars, on canvas, most vivid and accurately showing the stirring activity of the Battlefield conflicts, the successes of our troops in pacifying the American Indian and the wonderful advancement in their condition to-day. Your efforts and success in placing before the people these historical productions will be more fully appreciated when every actual participant in the field who made it possible for the Pioneer to cross and occupy the "great American Desert" west of the Missouri river, when, with the assertion positive to the opposite of any thing pessimistic will become the center of greatest production and political power of this great growing Empire.[33]

Cody celebrated the following days by reading more positive reviews from officials in the Wilson administration. If he read critiques of other Indian films, it may have heartened him to learn that the moving picture press regarded the battle scenes between troopers and Indians in the recently released Kalem company's film *The Big Horn Massacre*—similar to those of his own battle pictures—"highly exciting." The critic thought many "weak and sloppy" Indian films failed because they were "tame." Kalem's latest was "so savage, so vigorous in the quality of its action, because the camera shows 'stomach' in taking it." *Moving Picture World* reviewed another new film titled *Captured by Redskins*. The writer could have been talking about Cody's film: "Indian pictures exist chiefly for the animated action they make possible. It is the hard riding, the attack and battle, the capture and rescue that are expected in them. Yet the story is important too; but even where that is not strong, if the other items are present, the piece will be counted entertaining by many." On the other hand, only a month later, the news reported that fickle "audiences have felt the touch of progress and have consigned the 'Western' to oblivion; they demand newer and better things of the motion picture."[34]

Moving Picture World columnist Louis Reeves Harrison defined the "finest and final test of a screen story": The scenes may or may not be "true to life" or its characters "thoroughly natural," but if the story "revealed something spiritual, an idea that lives and breathes, a sentiment that grips the heart, a spark that sets the mind aflame," it was worthwhile.[35] It remained for audiences to decide if Cody's film measured up to those standards.

CHAPTER 9

Box Office Buzz

Until lions have their historians, tales of the hunt shall always glorify the hunters.

AFRICAN PROVERB

With government approval came lucrative offers from exhibitors, many of whom expected a New York City premier. Residents of Cody, Wyoming, hoped *The Indian Wars* would debut publicly in the town William Cody founded; but, despite initially planning to open in New York's Madison Square Garden "for real money," Cody eventually decided he owed the special favor to Denver. Almost certainly pressured by Tammen and Bonfils, he insisted that the pictures "must have their premier in the West . . . in the city that had made it possible for all this to be accomplished."[1]

Beginning March 8, 1914, the film ran in Denver's Tabor Opera House twice daily for a week. John Burke confided to the press at a private showing in the General Film Company's screening parlor that its realism moved him to tears. He spoke of overcoming his aversion to Indians and of having "formed a strong friendship for 'Poor Lo.'"[2] A self-described peacemaker, he reminisced about the women singing death songs during the 1890 battle, Forsythe arriving with the dead and wounded, the attacks on the wagon train and mission. In predicting the film would bring Cody "another fortune," Burke conceded Cody's advancing age but said youngsters could still see him, "a little disfigured but still in the ring, and proving that game birds can 'come back.'"[3]

During the two-and-a-half-hour screening, critic Frances Wayne found that "every second is one of breath suspended thrills." She commented on the "deep religious element" evident when the messiah appears "and leads them toward extermination." Like Jesus speaking on the mount, Wovoka spoke "from a towering cliff"—just one remarkable scene in the "splendid panorama of brave deeds, superb horsemanship, of nature in that violent, destructive mood." She continued, "Splendid drama is here, indescribable courage; craft, cunning, cruelty pitted against brains, experience, knowledge, science and in the end, those unforgettable tableaux." Despite the grim realism, she concluded, "no boy or girl should be allowed to miss these pictures. If you are a lonely man or woman pick up some equally lonely kiddie and take him for an afternoon with the great leaders of our army, with the great chiefs of our Indian tribes and two hours in the open world that has been made sacred by heroic blood of the nations' fighting heroes."[4]

Despite the film's historical relevance, social worker Jane Addams might disagree. She worried about children addicted to movies who could not separate the fantasy of film from reality. While imitating a cinematic stagecoach holdup, several young boys nearly killed a milkman. Playing soldiers and Indians could have similar disastrous consequences. As a result, by 1913 some states prohibited children from seeing films without an adult.[5]

The *Rocky Mountain News and Times* critic wrote of Cody's film that "nothing more picturesque, more thrillingly entertaining, was ever staged." He insisted that no artist could paint the picture and no historians could write the story of those days. It remained for the camera to capture the "vast open spaces, the wild land, which [God] heaved up on end, sternly forbidding, desolately

A reenactment of Wovoka prophesying on the mountain. (Buffalo
Bill Historical Center, Cody, Wyo., P.69.2067)

repelling." To bring home the human tragedy, "it needs the
solid phalanx of cavalry, drooping beneath the icy cold winds,
as, wrapped in their great-coats, they ride across the limitless,
snow-covered steppes of our mighty West. . . . It needs the
action, the terrorizing fight, the hand-to-hand conflict, the rush
and swirl, the clouds of smoke, the pitching forms of stricken
humanity, the sight of women and little children huddled in
tepee and ravine."[6]

Between reels, in a confluence of film and reality, Cody,
wearing the same jacket he wore in the film, galloped onto the
stage on his white horse. The audience burst into spontaneous
applause. Cody patted Isham and said, "Gee, old pard, that was
a hot one; we are going swift; two victories of forty-five and

A lone warrior lies on the battlefield. (Buffalo Bill Museum and Grave, Lookout Mountain, Golden, Colo.)

thirty-eight years ago in forty minutes, and another campaign to move on for," then he rode off past the footlights.[7]

Critic Hugh O'Neill wrote of the film's influence on his fellow viewers: As the Hotchkiss guns mowed down the Indians, "the man near me sucked the breath from between teeth and muttered, 'My God!' He twined and untwined his fingers. Another clapped his hand across his mouth to stifle a sob. Somebody groaned." As the on-screen Indians chose to fight rather than retreat, the battle scenes reflected "an afternoon of methodical, wholesale killing."

"I heard a man praying in whispers."

"We had them up against a wall and we were pounding them to pieces. Sometimes they formed and came charging down the hillside to the ravine as though thus to hasten death. And each time they charged our gunner found the range and they halted and spun round and fell as a stone falls when a shell burst above them. . . . It was killing reduced to a business."

The snow fell and the smoke hung heavy. A man gritted his teeth and muttered, 'My God! Why don't they surrender?' As if answering him, the bugles sounded 'Cease firing.'"[8]

Cody, Miles, and Wharton expected the chronicle to inspire such deep emotions. The realism transported viewers into the battle so that, at least momentarily, they forgot that the events had occurred decades earlier. When the lights came on, racing pulses, dry throats, and teary eyes remained. The film's intensity led to the conclusion that "it is War itself; grim, unpitying and terrible, [it] holds your heart still as you watch it and leaves you, in the end, amazed and spellbound at the courage and the folly of mankind."[9]

Curiously, Denver columnist Fay King reacted completely differently. She glibly described the action: When the Hotchkiss guns were turned on the Indians, "It kills 'em like flies!" When the soldiers force the Indians to surrender their arms, "one tough old buck reniggs and . . . in a jiffy that place is turned into a slaughter house. That field looked like a piece of fly paper on a hot day." Under military escort, there were "long parades of Indians in their gally-galorious costumes . . . with the fat, runny squaws trudging along, draggin' the wig wams behind them." At the Ghost Dance, "you ought to see them fat squaws do the Wig Wam Wiggle. I just sat there an' hollered. And the Costumes! . . . If you want to have new thrills, just set through that Indian [film]."[10]

On Saturday, March 14, the Grand Army of the Republic held its reunion in Denver and attended a presentation of *The Indian Wars.* "The boys in blue. The boys in gray. Both meeting under a common flag to celebrate the closing of warfare between the North American Indians and his conqueror, the white man," wrote Frances Wayne. When the performance concluded, Cody headed for Omaha to begin lecturing with the film.[11] He was thrilled with the enthusiastic response and telegraphed his hotel's manager to boast, "Splendid opening, two packed houses. Pictures received great ovation. Held two immense audiences spell-bound." When the news spread, the townspeople from Cody appealed for a showing by sending him a "good strong letter," suggesting the "general fitness of things" meant they should be able to view the film soon. Cody replied that the factory was working overtime to make copies for big cities, and he hoped to have twenty distributors out within the month.[12]

Fred Garlow was fortunate to distribute the film in Nebraska when its immediate popularity caused the price of states rights to increase.[13] The average wholesale cost of one reel—about 1,000 linear feet—was $100. Fortunately, by 1914, audiences favored feature films, that is, films of five reels or longer, and were willing to pay double the normal nickel admittance charge.[14] The film did only fair business in Blair, Nebraska, but Garlow hoped to show more strongly in Iowa. He headed to Wahoo, returned to Omaha, and from there to Hooper and Oakland. He ordered publicity proclaiming *The Indian Wars* "a Money-Maker . . . without an equal." Advertising posters on which large-font text announced that the "FIVE REEL FILM THAT WILL LIVE FOREVER" was available to exhibitors to "STOP THE CROWDS and get you the business—6 one-sheets, 3 three-sheets, 1 six-sheet, 2 eight sheets, 2 sixteen sheets."[15]

While in Nebraska, Garlow discovered an article in the *Omaha Daily News* that claimed Indians found the film "false and misleading." They vowed to petition Washington to suppress it. Joseph Horn Cloud and Iron Hail, participants in the filming, said the movie version showed Indians and soldiers "in equal force and the Indians in war paint. Instead, they declare, the Indians were taken by surprise, attacked by a superior force and massacred, both women and children being killed." Garlow, confused over why Iron Hail would say such things, sent the article to Pine Ridge agent John Brennan with a message that he felt the "whole thing is some personal greivence on the part of some one up there" at the agency. If Brennan believed the sentiment was widespread, Garlow would change his plans to show the film eventually in Pine Ridge or its vicinity. In the name of the Buffalo Bill Historical Moving Picture Company, he then also refuted the report that the pictures were exaggerated "for show purposes" in a letter to the Omaha editor.[16]

Brennan promptly replied that he was unaware of any Indian objections, especially since they had not yet seen the film. He assured Garlow that the article was not sent from Pine Ridge but guessed it was the same one various newspapers had published at the time of the filming. In conclusion, he was sure the Indians would be "very much pleased" to see the film soon.[17]

It was not the first protest brought to Brennan's attention. During filming, the *Omaha Bee* had published a lengthy letter from "Old Fogy," who claimed to be a friend of George Wallace, a captain killed in the original battle. Given Cody's career as a much-publicized showman, Old Fogy understood why he would "seek such notoriety" in connection with a film about Wounded Knee but confessed puzzlement over "an honored soldier"— General Miles—lending his support "to a palpable sham." Fogy pointed out that Big Foot, having women and children in tow, obviously did not plan for war, and he wondered why history needed to be "distorted."[18]

Warren Moorehead, a journalist at Pine Ridge in 1890, had sent Brennan a similar article. Moorehead wrote sympathetically about the Indians, the Ghost Dance, and the subsequent massacre, his thesis being that "Force caused Wounded Knee. Humanity would have prevented it."[19] Two months before he received Garlow's letter, Brennan had also told Moorehead there was no truth to it. Yes, Cody had assisted in the filming, but he did not pose for the camera; the generals remained at the agency and did not participate. Brennan himself was on the battlefield, so he knew whereof he spoke. He suspected that the articles were "fakes written by a disgruntled crank for the deliberate purpose of besmirching" the filmmakers and reiterated, "So far as I am aware, there was nothing wrong with the whole proceedings, except in the wild imagination of the author of the articles."[20]

Besides Old Fogy, reproach was not long in coming from Sioux spokesman Chauncey Yellow Robe. At a meeting of the Society of American Indians, he scorned Cody and Miles for mocking the events at Wounded Knee "for their own profit and cheap glory." To those who wonder how to settle Indian troubles, Yellow Robe suggested acerbically that the two "take some soldiers and go around the reservations and shoot them down" and accused them of wanting to be "heroes for moving pictures."[21]

Yellow Robe found fault with his people appearing in any kind of Wild West show. He blamed whites for thinking they were perpetuating Indian culture when they were only using Indians for entertainment. His people often needed the employment shows offered because of the life they were forced to lead, but he felt the influence of such shows did not lead the Indians to ideal citizenship. When news of the Ghost Dance reached him at the Indian school in Carlisle, Pennsylvania, he warned his father not to participate or to believe in the "new foolish Messiah. If you do you will be a bad fix." Cody and Miles's reenactment was fodder for his rage. *The Indian Wars*, he said, was "a disgrace and injustice to the Indian race."[22]

A few days after the publication of Yellow Robe's comments, the *Daily Star* of Lincoln, Nebraska, quoted Melvin R. Gilmore, curator of the Nebraska state historical museum and possibly the anonymous Old Fogy, who stated that the Wounded Knee battle scenes were "not truthful" and "distinctly unfair to the Indians." He had been in the crowd watching the reenactment and had had his ear to the ground as he lingered around the agency. He boasted to Clarence Paine, secretary of the Nebraska Historical Society, that he was "looking on with both eyes and listening with both ears" and concluded the film was "a financial scheme . . . under the pretense of representing history." He credited the Indians' participation because they sincerely wished to show they held no grudge, but most, trusting the film would show events fairly, were distressed, thinking they had been tricked into participating. Gilmore was secretive about his self-assigned mission, seeking no publication because he didn't want "to be queered with government powers."[23] He was "rather proud of this scoop," he wrote, when battle survivors told him they were handed as many munitions as the whites had for the film; they did what they were told, wore the feathers, blankets, and beads they were given, but "nothing was done right." They understood they were making a "sham battle," not a reproduction of Wounded Knee. After his interviews, Gilmore grew angrier with the government for "adding insult to injury" by endorsing the completed film.[24]

Both Miles and Baldwin sent Brennan a copy of Gilmore's remarks, and the tone felt similar to the article Garlow had sent him. Baldwin argued, "The Indians understood perfectly what they were doing."[25] Brennan cursed Gilmore as a "nature fakir from Lincoln" and suggested Miles contact the secretary of the Interior and the commissioner of Indian Affairs to rebut the article's falsehoods.[26] Philip Wells was equally outraged. "To deceive them all so completely as [Gilmore] states," Wells said, "would lead one to believe that we are living in the age of miracles."[27] Essanay manager Vernon Day remarked that someone was taking a lot of pains to give the project publicity; he knew the only nonauthentic part of the film was the nature of the slaughter, in which the audience does not see women and children being killed. When the press reported that the Sioux, perhaps riled by Gilmore, decided to send a committee to Washington to protest, Day suggested they come to Chicago first. "We might save them some money by ending their trip here rather than going to Washington under misapprehension."[28]

Cody remained apart from the fray and accompanied the film to Omaha to help with Nebraska promotions. Essanay had reedited the film to fit into approximately a two-hour time slot. Audiences generally found it truer to life than newspapers had led them to believe. The one "defect," critiqued the Omaha press, was the Indians' costumes. The fighting Indians had been "poor, half-starved creatures," but those same Indians, now better off, insisted on "'dressing up' for the occasion to the limit of their means" and appeared in the film "dressed in the costly and full regalia of Indian chiefs." The critic predicted the film would likely lead historians to research the cause of the wars. He reasoned that, if white men with no knowledge of farming had to subsist on a reservation's arid land and be reduced to starvation as were the Indians, they too might have gone to war.[29]

When the time came to pay the piper, Harry Tammen, Cody had to withdraw from promoting the film and climb back into the saddle as the number one feature of the Sells-Floto Circus. John Burke attempted to find the good in the situation, announcing,

"Col. Cody long has contemplated spending his later days as an educator in a manner to bring the context of western story in closer touch and more pleasant conditions to the little ones, and with enough ginger to please the middle-aged, and be of realistic reminiscences to the old-timers, pioneers and early settlers of the west. His choice fell upon the Sells-Floto show as the best medium, from its efficient organization."[30] He failed to mention that Cody was indebted by contract.

When Sells-Floto toured California, Cody visited director Sidney Ayres at the American Studio in Santa Barbara, indicating his continued interest in movie making.[31] Meanwhile, Garlow continued to plug the film in Nebraska, showing it in Chadron on April 19, 1914; North Platte on May 13 and 15; Alliance on May 15 and 16; and in Lincoln's Orpheum Theater May 21–23.[32] Reviewers called it "intensely dramatic" and "vividly interesting. . . . One readily forgives the anachronism of his white goatee and his famous, favorite white horse." During part of the newly revised film, audiences could watch the dedication of a monument marking the point at which the Oregon Trail crossed the Nebraska and Kansas state lines.[33] Another exhibitor booked it for a week at the Orpheum Theater in Des Moines, Iowa, May 10–17. Anticipation ran high when news spread of spectators' praises in cities where the movie had already been exhibited, including Brooklyn where it showed as *The Last Indian Rebellion*.[34]

In June 1914, the *Evening Wisconsin* reported that General King would lecture members of the press club about his Indian-fighting experiences, complete with accompanying illustrations. No doubt reporters asked about his role in Cody's film, but King continued to be abashed at the inference that he would engage in such self-aggrandizement. Unlike General Miles, whom one historian described as one of the "most ambitious and publicity-conscious officers ever to have worn Uncle Sam's blue," King was a modest man who applauded Cody's Indian wars project but removed himself from any glory affiliated with it. A few years

later, at Cody's funeral, King praised the aptitude that "especially endeared him to the officers and men whose business it
was to hunt down the Indians in the west. . . . [Cody] seemed to
know the Indian as no white man had known him up to his
time, and he could outwit him in almost every instance."[35]

To prove his support, when Cody's film showed in Milwaukee
during the week of July 6, 1914, King attended at least three
times. For a later issue of *Moving Picture World*, he contributed
his memories, recalling the soldiers' fourteen-mile march, the
wind-driven snow flying in their faces, and the soldier with two
fingers shot off "shouting that it was all dammed foolishness."
King said, "It was like some nightmare that we had been weeping
in through eternity."[36]

Continuing his tour, Garlow took the film to Decatur, Illinois,
for screenings at three separate theaters July 13–15. The Isis
Pure Air Theater in Cedar Rapids exhibited the film on July 29
and 30; the newspaper there inflated the film's cost to "hundreds
of thousands of dollars" but highlighted the settlers' "indescribable courage" and the "bloodthirsty cruelty of the savages . . .
portrayed in a manner that will leave no doubt as to the authenticity of the stories written about the Indian tribes." Garlow then
took the film to Oelwein, Iowa, on July 23 and to Carroll, Iowa,
on August 21.[37]

Meanwhile, though Cody's only duty with Sells-Floto was to ride
into the arena and salute the audience, he had an exhausting
summer. The outdoor season was over by the time his moving
pictures showed in Cody, Wyoming. Anticipation generated
record attendance and, because the film was "creating such a
sensation in big eastern cities," it was possible to exhibit it for
only one day with standing room at a premium for the two
showings. The audience felt honored to be the first in Wyoming
to see it, sitting enthralled throughout. Cody made his surprise
appearance before leaving for a recuperative rest and more
travel with the film.[38]

Reports of the film's presentation under sundry titles are scattered throughout contemporary newspapers. To appeal to local tastes, exhibitors might rename a film; thus *The Indian Wars* was also promoted as *Indian War Pictures, Last Indian Battles, Buffalo Bill's War Pictures, Indian Wars Refought by the U.S. Army, From the Warpath to the Peace Pipe,* and *The Wars for Civilization in America,* or any combination thereof. Because of Cody's contract with Pliny Craft, he could not title the film *The Life of Buffalo Bill* or *The Adventures of Buffalo Bill.* Thus, *Indian Wars Refought* showed in Los Angeles in mid-October 1914; six reels played in Perry, Iowa, in mid-November as *Buffalo Bill's Historical Pictures of Indian Battles Refought. Buffalo Bill's Wild West Circus,* the film, exhibited in Lacrosse, Wisconsin, on December 10, as his Indian wars picture showed in Fort Wayne, Indiana.[39]

Ads in *Moving Picture World* continued to cajole exhibitors by praising the film's "beautiful Photography and realistic Scenes" and asserting that "nothing more Picturesque, more thrillingly entertaining was ever staged. Nothing to equal it will, perhaps, ever be done again." Promotions called for exhibitors to contact these men for bookings in the respective states: F. W. Redfield for Georgia, Tennessee, Florida, Alabama, and the Carolinas; John F. Connolly for Montana, Utah, Wyoming, New Mexico, Colorado, and Nevada; Robert A. Brackett in California and Arizona; W. T. Norton for Washington, Oregon, and Idaho; and E. H. Painter for Ohio.[40]

From March 28 through April 1, 1915, the Wounded Knee portion showed in Denver at the Empress Theater with additional reels containing scenes of Cheyenne's Frontier Days, the town of Cody, and the Prince of Monaco's hunt. The press advertised these as "Buffalo Bill" pictures and also as a "Romantic Review of the Life of Buffalo Bill." Cody attended and promoted all of them after returning from a tour of Carl Laemmle's new Universal City movie metropolis in Los Angeles.[41]

There was, however, little news of the film only a year past its release except for a showing in Eau Claire, Wisconsin, July 19–20, 1915. It seemed Billings, Montana, was onto something with its Fourth of July observance titled "Passing of the West." The "Old west was passing into discard," read placards. New generations found the frontier only a memory replaced by "new work, new ambitions, new forms of play."[42]

Continued indenture to Harry Tammen and the Sells-Floto Circus left Cody little time for further lecturing and promotion. He was also preoccupied with other investments and construction projects: a canal, a dam, and a road into Yellowstone Park. But in the fall and winter of 1915/16, he and Johnny Baker traveled the New England states exhibiting the film in Springfield, Worcester, and Fall River, Massachusetts; Stamford, Bridgeport, New Haven, and Hartford, Connecticut; and throughout New York and Vermont. They were pleased when thousands of people flocked to the presentations. Baker believed *The Indian Wars* proved as celebrated and popular as the Wild West show had ever been.[43]

CHAPTER 10

Fade Out

I cannot separate the events of my life from the figure I became in the eyes of the world.

WILLIAM F. CODY

The eagerness with which many audiences received *The Indian Wars* at the outset could not countermand the myriad factors influencing its ultimate inefficacy. Despite Cody's foresight in capturing Old West images while they were still available for the capturing, the elaborate spectacle that was to serve as tribute to his role in settling the West, as a means of government recruitment for the imminent war, and as a documentary of the army's triumphant role in the Indian wars turned out to be a re-presentation of a too real, too painful, and too recent frontier past.

When circumstances forced him to forego the trappings of the Wild West arena for a scenic but brutal winter's battleground, Cody claimed the resultant moving pictures would corroborate actual events. His formerly successful arena show had also claimed historical accuracy, but the show's reenactments were merely reductions of complex historical events into easily perceptible scenes combining myth with sensational melodrama.[1] In filming the massacre at Wounded Knee, Cody misjudged the subtlety between scripted role-playing and reenacting from memory. Indian historian Vine Deloria, Jr., wondered if his reproducing the Wounded Knee battle on the same site "destroyed much of the good will that Cody had painstakingly earned over the decades."[2] He had never staged the 1890 battle in the Wild West show. Perhaps experiencing its failure there might have led him to reconsider it as a cinematic subject. Reproducing the cavalry's slaughter of American Indians emotionally exhausted all concerned but led many critics to praise the film's realism as "something we can never see again. The grim and grizzled participants are in the Christmas of their days; their race is nearly run; they can never again be actors on the stage as they were in this tremendous reproduction."[3] Watching it from a seat in a comfortable darkened theater could not diminish the horror or the realization that settling the nation had been a bloody and deadly affair.

Eager as he was to recoup his Wild West show's losses, nevertheless, as a novice filmmaker, Cody should have heeded the advice of the businessman familiar with moving pictures who said, "I don't believe that anyone should invest in the motion picture industry more than he can afford to lose. . . . [The industry] is always changing." Filmmaking existed to amuse a public notorious for its capriciousness, "this due in part to the fact that you tired of what the motion picture manufacturers were handing out, and in part to the fact that certain progressive manufacturers fertile in new ideas, gave you such novel and pleasing pictures that you would not stand for the old timers." He emphasized that "stocks of practically all movie concerns are business risks." Factoring in competition from Vitagraph's "Six [new films] a Week," Méliès's science fiction, Essanay's westerns, and comedies, mysteries, and religious-themed films from sundry filmmakers, even "hundreds of thousands of dollars . . . dumped into the business with a shovel" was no guarantee of future returns. *The*

Indian Wars competed with nearly 4,200 other films from 1913, many of them by imaginative directors unafraid to try innovative techniques in the telling of epic subjects.[4]

Moreover, Cody had disregarded film journalists who had long predicted that western photoplay was "slated for an early demise" similar to "the case of a gold mine that has been worked to the limit and can give no more desirable ore." *Moving Picture World* columnist Stephen Bush studied audiences in theaters where Indians were "doing their worst on the screen, and noticed no feverish enthusiasm denoting approval." As early as 1911, an exhibitor complained that he was "getting tired of shooting a couple hundred Indians every week, and both my operators and piano players are actually becoming saddle sore."[5]

Cody himself had little money invested; his contributions included time and effort spent touring with the film. Though experiences as a showman prepared him for public speaking, he confided to his sister, "Lecturing is a new game for me—But I believe I can do it."[6] No record exists of exactly what he said in his talks but, never reticent about offering his opinion, he may have included the following sentiments from his autobiography:

> I want to express the hope that the dealings of this Government of ours with the Indians will always be just and fair. They were the inheritors of the land that we live in. They were not capable of developing it, or of really appreciating its possibilities, but they owned it when the White Man came, and the White Man took it away from them. It was natural that they should resist. It was natural that they employed the only means of warfare known to them against those whom they regarded as usurpers. . . .
>
> The Indian makes a good citizen, a good farmer, a good soldier. He is a real American, and all those of us who have come to share with him the great land that was his heritage should do their share toward seeing that he is

dealt with justly and fairly, and that his rights and liberties are never infringed by the scheming politician or the shortsighted administration of law.[7]

Although *The Indian Wars* was more historical documentary than typical western, the effects of the overproduction of westerns worried potential film exhibitors and critics. Action-filled plots coupled with technical improvements were not sufficient to overcome the stale similitude, and they found reason to disparage his film in both genres. "Uniquely American" westerns full of guns and gore had too often offended some filmgoers with their wanton violence, while others found the dangers and the potential risk of pain or death appealing. Before censors squelched the gratuitous violence over worry that it might prove infectious, Stephen Bush found that westerns did foster "a spirit of roughness" in the rowdy male crowds who frequented them. Their unruliness frightened away higher-class people from the theaters "as if they were infested with the plague." Many plots derived from dime novels, which such theater patrons abhorred.[8] Thus, eager to attract customers expecting intelligent artistry, many exhibitors eliminated westerns from their programs.

By 1914, many of these same patrons had read about, or seen for themselves, films claiming to be newsreels or documentaries taken in the field of war and suspected that often what they saw instead was staged fiction. Jabez Cross, one participant of the Wounded Knee battle, scoffed at Cody's enactment. "He did not take any part in the fighting and was no more a hero of the war, as it is called, than [my friend E. N.] Todd or I was. . . . Anyway, it wasn't a battle and it wasn't a war. Wounded Knee was just a massacre and that's about all the fighting we had up there." Perhaps for this reason, audiences doubted the authenticity the promotions heralded, particularly when other studios frequently advertised their fictional features as "true to life."[9]

Cody's film did supply the action exhibitor Fred Jeffreys claimed his customers wanted but, although they had heard of historic events like Wounded Knee, the fall of Troy, or the beginnings of Christianity, many preferred "something of every-day life, something not too deep for them." Such patrons rarely considered documentaries entertaining, and they made westerns popular for their amusement, not didactic value. As film historian Kevin Brownlow remarked, "No one goes to a Western for a history lesson."[10] After a glut of western films that replicated the same scenes outdoor arena shows portrayed, one film journal argued for an "elevating educative trend," "something that will teach a good lesson and not leave a bad taste in the mouth with its many holdups, murders, and shootings."[11] Cody pronounced *The Indian Wars* instructive, but many filmgoers cared little for its intrinsic history.

The glut of new films in general shown in brand-new "million-dollar palaces" drew a new type of audience as well. The working class, who preferred pulps and "shockers" in serial format, as well as "the unwashed boys in the front seats" who preferred westerns, were no longer primary movie customers; instead, "the great middle class" favored comfort and fine presentations. When their tastes dictated a decrease in the production of scientific, travel, or industry-based films, informational movies became "decidedly unpopular." With little profit to be made, exhibitors and producers had to be "a Carnegie, a Rockefeller or a Sage" to engage in educational filmmaking.[12]

Moreover, the appeal of westerns conclusively declined when audiences discovered their "certain degree of sameness and monotony."[13] One journalist blamed Cody's retirement for the waning interest in American Indians and cowboys. At the time he was perpetuating past battles, Americans anticipated the country's participation in a future war. Young boys abandoned cowboys and Indian fighters as heroes in favor of submarine navigators or airplane pilots.[14] The "war to end war" made headlines,

and the public demanded all the pictorial war news available—
not Indian wars over for nearly a quarter century but events
from the European front. "The Great War was too large, too
spectacular, and too dramatic an event not to be exploited,"
observed one historian, and filmmakers hastened to produce
newsreels of field engagements, many of which they faked when
the government prohibited filming the military in action.[15] But,
unlike the Civil War, which continued to be a popular subject,
particularly at its fiftieth anniversary, the draw of martial films
lapsed when the war in Europe ended. Moreover, when paying
for the conflict caused the cost of living to skyrocket, both productions and attendance declined.[16]

The appeal of cinematic Indians, as necessary an element in
westerns as cowboys, also tapered off. Nearly 150 Indian films
were made in 1914, about forty-five were produced in 1915, and
that number decreased to fewer than twenty-five the next year.[17]
Because of Cody's promise to show Indians' progress in order
to pacify the Bureau of Indian Affairs, his otherwise war-filled
film concluded rather anticlimactically. Sympathizers who might
have promoted Cody's film to fuel support for Indian rights
found that World War I ended much of the country's idealism
toward its first inhabitants.

Another factor inhibiting interest in Cody's film was its length.
Versions varied from five, six, to eight reels, with times ranging
from approximately one and a quarter hour to the longest lasting
nearly two and half hours. Shortly after *The Indian Wars* was
released, no less an innovator than Carl Laemmle, a founder of
Universal Studios, predicted that "long features are doomed."
His comment was, however, no doubt a reaction to the accomplishments of his competitor, Adolph Zukor, chairman of Paramount studio who was generally credited with inaugurating
feature films onto America's cinematic scene. Exhibitors hoped
manufacturers would return to single or double features ("shorts")
when patrons complained that five- and six-reel features were

too long. Seventy minutes was about as long as most preferred to spend watching a film. *Motion Picture News* considered two reels "full value received," and three reels were "a plenty for five cents." *Moving Picture World* argued that length shouldn't matter as long as the story was well told with a satisfactory ending, but it acknowledged that few producers could fill 1,000 feet with excitement. One journalist posited that "the single reel will, so far from becoming less important from now on, become more and more important"—a prediction not fulfilled, as feature-length films became the norm by 1915.[18]

One practical reason audiences desired shorter features might simply have been the chairs they sat in and the air they breathed. When the Strand opened in New York City in 1914, it was an elaborate moving picture house, having a tasteful interior of rose, gray, and gold. Murals covered the walls, and "changed" air blew through a perforated dome. Primitive air conditioning cooled patrons via a blower system, and valves under the plush seats heated the air in winter. Countless theaters, however, offered little or no ventilation. Stale air induced headaches, and the chairs were often of hard wood on iron or steel bases with wrought iron arms. One thoroughly uncomfortable-looking model with no armrests balanced on a pedestal-style base.[19]

Despite what he may have read in the trade papers, Cody was positive *The Indian Wars* would do well. After all, the construction of ten thousand movie theaters by 1910 proved film had become one of the most popular forms of commercial entertainment.[20] But one thing he could not predict was popular tastes. A generation of aging Wild West audiences who had seen the vibrant, youthful Buffalo Bill simply may have been indifferent to an elderly Cody, no matter the venue. Younger western stars like Broncho Billy Anderson, Tom Mix, and William S. Hart caused bigger sensations at the box office.

Too, generations of the late nineteenth and early twentieth centuries lived through amazingly innovative times. Scott Joplin popularized a new music form called ragtime that energized nightclubs and speakeasies and reached its height between 1913 and 1915, the very years Cody was promoting his film. Automobiles, formerly a luxury only the wealthy could afford, became available to the middle class. In-home radios providing news and entertainment were just over the horizon.

After war-themed pictures, athletics provided the focus for a large number of films. Moving pictures featured virtually every sport, from America's Cup yacht races to intercollegiate track meets, basketball games, and automobile races. It is possible that the camera stand Theodore Wharton used to oversee the Wounded Knee reenactment had been perfected for the 1910 World Series.[21] But Americans were not just watching filmed sports. They gathered in newly constructed grandstands and stadiums to cheer on their favorites in football games and tennis matches. Major league baseball clubs built parks catering to men fond of alcohol and gambling. Golf courses were accessible for those with leisure time and wherewithal to afford membership. For intellectuals, troupes of speakers and musicians presented Chautauquas and offered a wide variety of performances. Amusement parks prospered during the summer months.[22] Vaudeville continued to feature a mixed bag of entertainment from singers and dancers to comedians and magicians.

Finally, a theory regarding the commercial failure of *The Indian Wars* has been bandied about that, upon reflection, government officials decided the film was simply too realistic and did not show the military (or its commanders) in a favorable light. Film historian William K. Everson wrote that epic westerns must "be able to feed off feelings of patriotism, pride in accomplishment, and a sense of national progress and unity."[23] Instead, Cody's interpretation of Wounded Knee might invite concerned audiences—including influential politicians or historians—to revisit and investigate the events of 1890, a possibility conflicting with the goals of a government eager to insinuate that it had subdued and assimilated American Indians through peaceful means. If audiences viewed *The Indian Wars* as a biopic, Cody's actual presence in it left little doubt its account was valid. Unwilling to rebut Cody's version because of his legendary status, officials may have found the film too worrisome and called for its suppression. Thus, speculations abound that agents at the Bureau of Indian Affairs destroyed the film as early as the 1920s.[24]

For these reasons, the film's failure to increase Cody's coffers substantially left him no choice but to fulfill his contract with Harry Tammen. For two years he toured unhappily with Sells-Floto. Despite his inability to ride and shoot as in his grander days, an advertising poster depicted a white-haired, goateed Cody in a buckboard under the slogan "Buffalo Bill 'Still Holds the Reins,'" because his very presence helped fill grandstands.

The auction of all Wild West show trappings should have satisfied Tammen for the $20,000 Cody borrowed in January 1913, but Tammen's contention that "lawyers and thieves had gotten away with all the money" kept Cody on the hook. Thoroughly disgusted with the businessman, Cody became so distraught that he wrote a friend, "Although I avoided killing in the bad old days, I was prepared to kill Tammen." Faithful to his word, however, he stayed until the end of the season in October 1915.[25]

When he was finally out from Tammen's clutches, he hired out again, still trying to raise money to reinvent his Wild West show. He joined the Miller Brothers' 101. For them, he essentially performed the same services as for Tammen, but it was a happier time and lucrative for all parties. Tammen, however, would not let go and tried to stop Cody from using *The Indian Wars*, so Cody said, and threatened to sue for any profits he made touring with it. Even his former partner, Pawnee Bill Lillie, insisted that Cody "try to fix up some way with Tammen and stop him using your name, picture, and any one made up as you." George Spoor finally convinced Tammen to desist.[26]

Cody seemed excited about lecturing with the film on a month-long eastern tour beginning in New York in February 1916. While at his nephew's home in New Rochelle, he began a series of biographical articles William Randolph Hearst asked him to write. Later published in Hearst's magazine and used as the basis for several cinematic westerns, they told of "The Great West That Was: 'Buffalo Bill's' Life Story.'" In 1920 they were organized as his final autobiography. The tales are full of his encounters with Indians, but he did not mention his role in the moving pictures of the last Indian battles, which would continue to cause a commotion even after his death.

CHAPTER 11

Final Scenes

If he had died a little sooner he wouldn't have had to endure all these new things. But we two, we're a pair of nineteenth century boys who just happened to live too long.

MAJOR JOHN BURKE

Members of the press often asked Buffalo Bill what he would do when he retired. As president of the Campo Bonito Mining and Milling Company, the Southern Belle Mining Company, and Shoshone Irrigation Company, owner of the Irma Hotel, Pahaska Tepee, and Wapiti Inn, as well as proprietor of North Platte farms and cattle ranches, Cody wasn't sure he ever would, or could, retire.[1] Advancing age and ill health had not kept him from implementing schemes to reclaim his fortunes with moving pictures. He appeared in other films as well, perhaps planning to create a cinematic biography.

At the time of *The Indian Wars*, Henry Ford of automobile fame also realized the value of moving pictures and used them, not only to train his workers but also to convey news of the day to the public. He distributed "The Ford Animated Weekly"—a series of short newsreels—to any theater manager who requested them. In extant snippets of an episode titled "A day with the Wild West show," Cody communicates in sign language with Iron Tail, workers use a power driver to pound in tent stakes, and bucking broncos cavort on Wild West show grounds.[2]

Before the emergence of spaghetti westerns—those produced more cheaply in European countries like Italy than in the American West—Polish filmmaker Josef Klyk made "kielbasa westerns" combining Polish and American history. In 1914, capitalizing on Cody's popularity, he staged the showman standing under a sign advertising his "Farewell Appearance." In one scene, Cody walks into a saloon and poses under a poster of himself.[3]

When Cody had first asked permission to film on the Pine Ridge reservation, he promised to donate a copy of the film to the Interior and War departments. Two years after its completion, E. J. Ayers, chief clerk of the Interior Department, wrote to remind him of this. Cody confidently replied that he had already taken them to Washington—his biographer Nellie Snyder Yost believes he did this before he returned home for Christmas 1913—and called at Interior secretary Franklin Lane's office.[4] His excuse for the delay—"I was in the west"—does not explain why he didn't wait to deliver the film while in Washington for the February 1914 presentations. Lane was not in, so he had called on War secretary Lindley Garrison and left the reels with Garrison's secretary, who promised to notify Lane of the reels for Interior. Cody suggested that, if Ayers just communicated with Garrison's secretary, he "will find everything allright."

Ayers understood that the War Department had obtained six reels from Cody, had claimed entitlement to them under its agreement with the film company, and would not surrender them to the Interior Department. Essanay Film Company "through carelessness or cussedness," Cody guessed, had sent only one set, and he offered to bring the matter to the company's attention. Perhaps not trusting Cody to follow through, Ayers also wrote to Essanay.[5]

Vernon Day responded that they had furnished a set of films to Cody for the War Department. Essanay president George

Spoor, Day alleged, "knows nothing about any further promises made." When Day tossed the ball back to Ayers, suggesting he take up the matter with Cody, Ayers invited Cody to "straighten out the matter, which you heretofore so kindly promised to do." Biographer Richard Walsh stated that Cody "soon sold outright his interest in the Indian war films" but did not reveal when or to whom he sold.[6] It appears, however, that Cody lost interest in the project. He replied to Ayers, "If the Co dont carry out their obligations I'll pay personally for a set of Reels." In the final correspondence on record, Ayers noted "with gratification" that the Interior Department would "appreciate an early delivery of the same."[7]

That delivery never arrived. On January 10, 1917, William Frederick Cody died in Denver at the home of his sister.

Less than one month after his death, the Col. W. F. Cody Historical Picture Company, whose officers included Spoor, Johnny Baker, Harry Tammen, and Fred Bonfils, released a film initially titled *The Life of Buffalo Bill*, essentially another version of *The Indian Wars*. As was Spoor's custom, the pictures had been "rearranged," and the new copies were distributed through the Kleine-Edison-Selig-Essanay (K-E-S-E) service.[8] To avoid confusion with the 1912 O'Brien film of the same name, it was quickly renamed *Adventures of Buffalo Bill*. The company first permitted the Orpheum and Keith's circuit of film distributors to show the film in more than fifty theaters in the country's largest cities. Extensive advertising promised its "thrilling action, terrifying Indian battles and prairie skirmishes, its exciting moments contrasting with its acute pathos, its light, amusing situations fitting in consistently with the daring and dangerous humor of the grim frontiersmen." In seventy minutes, Cody appears as mail rider, buffalo hunter, and army scout. Scenes from his Indian wars picture fill the middle, then "intimate glimpses" of Cody at home and on hunting expeditions, including him guiding the Prince of Monaco, end the film.[9]

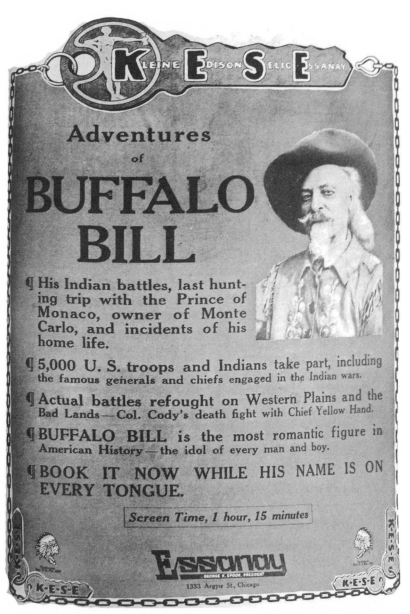

Adventures of Buffalo Bill advertised in *Moving Picture World*, Feb. 10, 1917.

At the end of January 1917, the picture exhibited in Rochester, New York, which held a special regard for Cody as a former resident. The press made much of his friendship with Spoor as showmen in different fields of entertainment. Cody, it reported, was "getting pretty old" at the time of the film taking, and "he had his own big affairs to look after, so he was rather averse to entering the picture." However, it alleged, Spoor convinced him of the importance of his participation, with the result that Cody and Miles "stand out as heroes on the film."[10]

After Cody's death, filmmakers discovered profit in palming off their products as "Buffalo Bill" pictures. Over the course of his show business career, Cody had been no stranger to the courtroom, and his death did not end legal squabbles over his name and character. In 1922, Universal Film Manufacturing Corporation produced an eighteen-chapter series titled *In the Days of Buffalo Bill.* The story of western history from 1861 to 1869 by Robert Dillon depicted Abraham Lincoln, Sitting Bull, Ulysses S. Grant, and John Wilkes Booth among other historical figures. According to the Cody company, a "spurious imitation and simulation" of Buffalo Bill, played by Duke R. Lee, appeared in nearly every episode.[11]

From July 29, 1922, until January 6, 1923, Universal persistently promoted the serial with ads and plot summaries in its weekly journal for film exhibitors. It sent Lee out on a personal tour to talk about picture making, and theater managers predicted it would be a "complete 'mop-up.'" One critic believed it would do well because it was "entertainment with a purpose." *Moving Picture World* congratulated director Edward Laemmle for the "historically correct scenes" as well as the "well staged action," and *Billboard* thought its educational value "unlimited." The drama, the trade magazine raved, wove historical events into a "romance with strong heart appeal."[12]

Throughout Universal's film, "Buffalo Bill" was ubiquitous. In the advertising, the words "In the Days of" were printed in "small,

"Crowds enough to fill a house three times as large!"

"WAITING crowds outside with lobby jammed two hours before the usual first show. Compelled to open at noon. By 2 o'clock had one full show played, with crowds waiting outside for the second show, large enough to fill a house three times as large as ours. It is one of the BIGGEST BOX-OFFICE ATTRACTIONS EVER MADE!"

Albert Dobbs,
EMPIRE THEATRE,
MILWAUKEE.

ART ACORD

and a wonderful cast of favorite players in the Greatest box-office attraction ever released as a continued feature

CARL LAEMMLE
presents

" In the Days of

Buffalo Bill"

Story by Robt. Dillon   Directed by EDWARD LAEMMLE

UNIVERSAL'S AMAZING CHAPTER PLAY

In the Days of Buffalo Bill advertised in *Universal Weekly*, Oct. 21, 1922.

insignificant letters" and "Buffalo Bill" blazed in a large font. Officers of Cody Historical Pictures petitioned the court for a temporary injunction to restrain Universal from using Cody's name or likeness in their marketing while attempting to show that *they* possessed exclusive right to the name even though Cody had not assigned any exclusivity or trademark he owned of his name.[13] Their argument regarding his omnipresence was undeniable:

Cowboy actor Art Acord playing Art Taylor, along with Bill Cody (Duke Lee), observes an Indian attack on Mr. Carter and his daughter Alice as they travel west by prairie schooner. Art rescues them while Cody rides to Fort Kearney for military support. The Carters take shelter in an abandoned shack, which the Indians attempt to set afire. Cody and the cavalry arrive to scatter them. The Carters turn the shack into a home, not knowing the land is proposed for a railroad junction. Meanwhile, in the East, thieves steal Granville Dodge's plans for the Union Pacific railroad, then offer to buy the Carters' now valuable land. They refuse. The villains try several plans to coerce the Carters off, including a fire and an explosion. In subsequent episodes, Art and Cody are accused of being spies for the Confederacy (or the Union), are sentenced to die and remarkably escape, or are fighting villains. They become Pony Express riders, Indian scouts, and buffalo hunters. Interspersed through the narrative, national events move the timeline along. Confederates and Union soldiers clash near the Carters' cabin as Sitting Bull's Sioux wage war against invading whites. In the episode in which Cody rescues Alice from Indians, Lincoln is assassinated. In the next, John Wilkes Booth is hunted down and killed. When Alice's father dies, Art and Alice appeal to Washington to keep the Carter homestead. Back in the West, in a foiled kidnapping, Alice falls off a cliff. During the rescue, Cody becomes trapped on a ledge, hanging by his fingers. Finally, all nefarious plans come to light and, in a happy ending, Alan Pinkerton seeks punishment for

the villains; the Golden Spike connects the rails; and Art, Alice,
Cody, and his fiancée marry in a double wedding.[14]

Over the course of judicial arguments, a defense attorney for
Universal Film interviewed Pliny Craft, who stated that he had
produced *The Life of Buffalo Bill* under the approbation of the
Buffalo Bill and Pawnee Bill Film Company and for which Cody
personally posed. Craft subsequently recut the film, added new
scenes, and reissued it as a two-reeler titled *In the Days of Buffalo
Bill.* He eventually sold it to a Frank A. Tichenor but kept an
interest in it as security for payment. Craft also claimed that he
retained the rights to use the title "Buffalo Bill" under his original
1910 contract with Cody and did not believe the plaintiff, Cody
Historical Pictures, had any exclusivity. At first Craft had no
interest in testifying for the defendant Universal, saying "his
personal interests would be better served if the plaintiff were to
succeed," but he could be coerced if Universal Film would buy
his rights to the name "Buffalo Bill" for $3,500. Presumably, since
his affidavit is included in the official record, Craft got his price.[15]

To further cloud the issue, Pawnee Bill Lillie, former partner
in their joint western show, also claimed ownership of the names
"Wm. F. Cody" and "Buffalo Bill." Noticing the extensive advertising for Universal's film, he instructed the company that, if
they desired to continue to use either, he would be happy to
make "amicable arrangements" and threatened legal action if
settlements were not forthcoming. Universal dismissed Lillie's
claim as "extraordinary" and "untenable."[16]

Louis Levand, assistant secretary of the Cody organization,
contended that Essanay, on behalf of the company, had copyrighted the photoplay *The Adventures of Buffalo Bill (Col. Wm. F.
Cody)* in five reels. Thorwald Solberg, register of copyrights, had
received two copies on January 25, 1917, according to papers in
Levand's possession. But in defendant's Exhibit S, Solberg cer-
tified that a careful search revealed no assignments to Essanay

for *The Adventures of Buffalo Bill* and no clue in the name of the Cody Historical Pictures Company. Levand added that the Cody Picture Company was "preparing to manufacture a large number of duplicate films and reels" in order to continue to exhibit the Buffalo Bill films on an even larger scale.[17]

No evidence existed to prove that calling their film a "Buffalo Bill" picture was any sort of copyright issue, rebutted Universal's lawyers, despite the fact that their advertisements in *Universal Weekly* promised a personal appearance by "Buffalo Bill." After all, they continued, *In the Days of Buffalo Bill* covered an epoch of history, whereas *The Adventures of Buffalo Bill* limited itself to one individual's deeds.[18] Besides, before William Frederick Cody became known as *the* Buffalo Bill, there were several "Buffalo Bills" in the West during the 1850s and 1860s. Stories and plays frequently included the name without Cody's consent or license. In 1872 when Cody attended the melodrama *Buffalo Bill*, he did not object to the use of his name in its title. Universal Pictures also insisted that its advertising made it perfectly clear Duke Lee played the part.[19] With a promotional budget of $157,000, Universal further explained that extensive promotion of its film would also benefit the popularity of the plaintiff's film—although in the opinion of John Broughton, general manager of Colonial Amusement Company and one of the defendants, an action picture "ceases to be commercially profitable from one to five years after its production."[20]

When the Cody Historical Picture Company argued its film's already protracted popularity and cited the numerous times it had shown in Denver's Empress Theater, the Universal Company belittled the vaudeville house as a place where motion pictures are "secondary and incidental" and termed such showings "casual, intermittent, interrupted, slight, tentative, incipient, and experimental." Generally, films shown there left little or no impression on the public.[21] Universal pounced on George Spoor's testimony that Essanay had rephotographed some scenes from the original film as proof it was "defective and such a failure" and suggested that the Cody company "intends at some future time to try it out again on some part of the unsuspecting public, probably sugar-coated with vaudeville."[22]

In the end, New York Supreme Court Judge John F. Symes ruled against the Cody Historical Picture Company on several points, remaining unconvinced that the movie-going public associated the name "Buffalo Bill" with the motion pictures of any particular company, thus ruling out the complaint of unfair competition. He also disregarded the copyright argument because the "title was copyrighted by a stranger to this record, and [there is] no proof that the name has been assigned to the complainant." He decided that, if a name such as Cody's becomes known in a business "with the assent and acquiescence of its creator, he cannot thereafter assert his right to its exclusive use." If Cody did intend that, it was too late now for anyone else to declare it on his behalf.[23] His ruling allowed the character "Buffalo Bill" to continue as a symbol of the great American west, but one not necessarily belonging to William Frederick Cody.

Over the years, various researchers have attempted to track down prints of the films in which Cody himself takes part. The Buffalo Bill Historical Center at Cody, Wyoming, kept copies, but in the early twentieth century the Center environment was not suited to preservation.[24] Fluctuating vault temperatures led to disintegration of nearly all of the original nitro-cellulose (nitrate) film. Storage of nitrate film, essentially a form of gun-cotton used in nearly all silent films, was, in fact, dangerous because it was prone to combustion. Early projectionists, aware of this trait, kept the film constantly running at least twelve frames per second past the hot projection lamp. Whether it took ten or fifty years, however, the footage would eventually grow gelatinous and emit potentially noxious bubbles of brown foam before drying to a powder.[25]

Files at the Buffalo Bill Center include a July 1930 letter from Mrs. Roza I. Odell of New Rochelle, New York, a wife of Cody's cousin, in which she queried the Interior Department about the reels. Then chief clerk W. B. Acker replied that their records "fail to show that any such films were filed in this Dept by Col. Cody." In addition, Acker wrote, for lack of funds the War Department had declined to purchase a film of the life of Buffalo Bill offered by the Buffalo Bill and Pawnee Bill Film Company in 1910. When the National Archives was established in 1934, no prints of *The Indian Wars* were available from the War or Interior departments. The Archives does hold a 1919 memo from C. F. Hauke, chief clerk of the Bureau of Indian Affairs, stating that the Bureau owned only one film but it was not Cody's.[26]

Bob Lee, former editor of *The Black Hills Historian*, had obtained a 1919 Interior Department memorandum noting that "the print was already in poor condition, with broken sprockets, cloudiness and brittleness." Unfortunately, in 2009 his widow was unable to locate the memo. However, Lee's claim to its existence indicates that the department had obtained its copy, but the film's condition made it worthless. In 1969, for a series of articles in the *Rapid City Journal*, Lee contacted the Library of Congress and verified that it had no copy of the film.[27]

In 1959, Blackhawk Films released a print of the 1912 O'Brien-directed *Life of Buffalo Bill*, a copy of which the Buffalo Bill Historical Center owns. Other original Cody footage in the Center's collection came from various sources: reels of 16 mm Wild West footage once belonging to Cody's daughter Irma Garlow. His niece, Mary Jester Allen, owned the Ford Motor Company scenes and also kept some footage of *The Indian Wars* in a safe deposit box. Former curator Dick Frost remembered that, when the film was checked in the 1950s, it had mostly decomposed. Technicians salvaged what they could on 16 mm safety film and spliced it with a conglomeration of Wild West show footage. The scenes include Buffalo Bill in Cody, Wyoming, in a parade on Sheridan Avenue, and at the DeMaris Hot Springs.[28]

In 1960, Hiram S. Cody, Buffalo Bill's distant nephew, contacted Kern Moyse, president of the Peerless Film Processing

Corporation, who quoted a price of $.065/foot to make a positive duplicate of original Cody film. The "delicate operation" required the company to build a special machine to shrink and restore the old reels. Moyse was then to preserve the 1,200 feet of negatives in his fireproof and air-conditioned vault. A 2009 search for the Peerless Film Company was not successful but, by interesting coincidence, "Peerless Film Manufacturing Company" was the name Spoor and Anderson considered before combining their initials into S'n'A (Essanay).[29]

Could *The Indian Wars* have been destroyed because of its inflammatory content or simply as a safety measure because of its nitrate base? Despite their value as historic artifacts, many films once stored at the Library of Congress were filed, then forgotten. Charles Grimm, film historian, reports seeing an article in a Washington, D.C., newspaper in the mid-1930s titled "Early Movies Rot in Cellar, Priceless Records of a Great Industry Filed Away in Dusty Obscurity."[30] To add to the bleakness, the Library's National Film Preservation Board concludes, "fewer than 20% of American silent films still survive in complete form; and for American films produced before 1950, half no longer exist."[31]

As early as 1915, cinematic specialists contemplated how to preserve film that had captured historic, never-to-be-repeated events and considered establishing an archive for the availability of such films for the indefinite future. However, chemical changes in the emulsion shortened its lifespan, and some museums refused to store nitrate film because its flammable nature required specially constructed vaults. In addition, scientists found that a fungus often grew on film stored in an airtight vault and untouched for years; therefore, they dismissed the idea of preserving films indefinitely as an impossibility.[32]

When Essanay went out of business, the company offered employees the opportunity to take anything they wanted. One man helped himself to original nitrate film negatives and movie prints. Years later, he contacted David Phillips of Chicago, a collector of old glass photographic negatives, and told him he was welcome to them. Phillips found a reel showing Miller 101 ranch activities with Cody, as well as the scenes of Prince Albert and Chief Plenty Coups and shots of Camp Monaco in the Rockies. Phillips gently cleaned the footage and sent it to a friend at a movie lab in New York. Fearful the original would combust, the friend carefully printed 16 mm and 35 mm positive and negative prints and returned it. A short time later, when Phillips opened the film can, he found only brown dust.[33] Prints at the Buffalo Bill Historical Center show Cody in white shirt and vest sitting on the lawn playing cards. When two more men join the game, "they make it four handed." The action switches to something not "nearly as exciting as fighting Indians"—pitching horseshoes on the side lawn.[34]

What remains of *The Indian Wars*, besides several still photographs, is a grainy three-minute snippet that is frustratingly fractured. In it, Cody appears to be scouting, then leading dark-uniformed cavalry over hilly country. Lying on his belly to peer over a ridge, he indicates to the soldier next to him his intention to change position. Cody and four soldiers ride to the base of the ridge, dismount, and the sixty-six-year-old Cody climbs to the rim again. The scene abruptly switches to Cody in a buggy, presumably on his way to talk to Sitting Bull. A messenger has caught up to him and hands off a note calling him back.[35]

Nearly a century after his death, it is impossible to guess whether there will ever be another film highlighting Buffalo Bill's legend. The spate of westerns in general, once so well received by the film-going public, has steadily decreased over the ensuing years, with only occasional bouts of popularity. Producer Kirk Ellis observed that westerns appear to have limited interest, "when in fact, it is a genre of universal appeal, not only within the United States, but also internationally."[36] With his cadre of Indians, Cody was one of the first to prove that.

CHAPTER 12

The Show Goes On

Cody's Character in Film

> *There isn't a single aspect of the history, philosophy, and psy-chology of film that hasn't been poked, prodded, dissected with a scalpel, or bludgeoned beyond recognition with a blackjack. Film by decade, by year, by subject, by director, by actor, by character, by phile and phobia, by genre, by context, by politics, by cinema-tographer, by caterer, subdivided by individual food issues.*
>
> LOREN ESTLEMAN, *ALONE* (2011)

After William Frederick Cody's death in 1917, western filmmakers continued to capitalize on his persona in their roster of themes. His presence in the cast, whether as protagonist representing the traditional western hero or as a minor participant in his-tory, gave credence to story lines built around land grabbers, Indians, railroad opponents, the Pony Express, wagon trains, and outlaws. Because he and most authentic frontiersmen had died, it was not necessary to keep to historical accuracy. History could serve merely as inspiration.

For example, in 1926, Jack Hoxie, "a beefy, amiable cowboy," played Cody in *The Last Frontier*, a project proposed by Thomas Ince. In the script, based on a Ryley Cooper story, Sioux chief Pawnee Killer attacks a wagon train led by Wild Bill Hickok and Beth Halliday's fiancé Tom Kirby. Hickok tells Cody about the assault. Beth, angry at Tom, whom the survivors suspect was in cahoots with the Sioux, joins a trader's household, and Tom signs on with Custer's expedition. With Custer in pursuit, the Sioux stampede a buffalo herd through town. At the conclusion, Pawnee Killer slays Beth's employer, and she and Tom are reunited.[1]

Though historians argue over whether Cody really did ride for the Pony Express, the 1860s' short-lived mail transport system lent itself to several cinematic interpretations. William Everson called James Cruze's *The Pony Express* (1925) "overlong and dull" and "a commercial disappointment," but Cruze, once the highest paid director, successfully captured the courage and hardships of a mail rider. In this romance, one ambitious senator secretly supports pro-slavery policies. He spearheads efforts to force California to secede, annex Mexico, and form a new country. His nemesis, gambler Jack Weston, foils a scheme by the senator's murderous henchmen and becomes a Pony Express rider. In this film, as in the next, a "Bill Cody" character is cast, but the role is so small as not to rate a mention in reviews.[2]

Early in 1938, Universal began production of *Outlaw Express* wherein U.S. cavalryman Bob Bradley and his sidekick go undercover to discover why many Pony Express riders, carrying recorded Spanish land grants from California to Washington, are being killed. Bradley guesses that Yankee outlaws are plotting to take over the land and kill the riders to steal the grants. His ability to "warble, fight rustlers, and romance with equal abandon" appealed mainly to youngsters.[3]

Universal hired John Rutherford to portray Cody in its 1938 *Flaming Frontiers* in another combination land grab/Pony Express script based on Peter Kyne's adventure story *The Tie That Binds*. This time the riders die at the hands of Indians. Rider Tex Houston (Johnny Mack Brown) meets Mr. Grant and his children on his mail route. Villain Bart Eaton plans to wed Mary Grant and steal her brother's mine. Filmmakers used serials, like this one in which the story line was broken into short segments, even in the silent era, and they remained a popular form of

moving pictures, especially westerns, in the early twentieth century. Cliffhangers ended each episode, guaranteeing audiences
would return the following week to see its resolution. Over the
fifteen weeks of *Flaming Frontiers,* Tex confronts Indians and
outlaws in order to save Mary and the mine. The episode titles,
typically a short, snappy phrase or snippet of dialogue, are 1, "The
River Runs Red"; 2, "Death Rides the Wind"; 3, "Treachery
at Eagle Pass"; 4, "A Night of Terror"; 5, "Blood and Gold";
6, "Trapped by Fire"; 7, "The Human Target"; 8, "The Savage
Horde"; 9, "Toll of the Torrent"; 10, "In the Claws of the Cougar";
11, "The Half Breed's Revenge"; 12, "The Indians Are Coming";
13, "The Fatal Plunge"; 14, "Dynamite"; and 15, "A Duel to the
Death."[4] Four years later, *Overland Mail* (1942) had Bob Baker
playing Cody the rider. A renegade disguises himself and his gang
as Indians in order to carry out raids on innocent settlers.[5]

In *Cody of the Pony Express* (1950), Dickie Moore had the title
role. When a crooked lawyer attempts to gain control of a terri-
tory by taking over its transportation routes, Cody joins an army
undercover agent to discover who's raiding the stagecoaches.[6]
Mail delivery returned to the theaters in 1953 with Charlton
Heston as "the most macho" Cody in the similarly titled *Pony
Express,* a remake of Cruze's film. He teams up with Wild Bill
Hickok to combat a brother/sister team intent on preventing
California from joining the Union. Cody fights off his old enemy
Yellow Hair as he and Hickok attempt to establish a pony express
system. Despite devious schemes, beautiful scenic shots, and
"tight western action," the film proved no more exciting than
the 1925 version.[7]

Cowboy crooner Roy Rogers personified Cody in *Young Buffalo
Bill* (1940). With sidekick Gabby Hayes, Rogers saves the day as
he sings his way through the hour-long Republic film. The script
has New Mexico landowner Don Regas trying to hold onto his
land with its lost mine despite nefarious schemes of his foreman

and his Indian cohorts. Regas's greenhorn son, a surveyor, figures in the plot. After a rout involving marauders and the cavalry, his son admits he erred on the survey, and Regas is awarded clear title to the land.[8]

Railroad history proved a fascinating cinematic subject in *The Iron Horse* (1925). A short biographical sequence recalls Cody's early career of supplying railroad workers with buffalo meat. Through twelve reels, the writers coupled the transcontinental railroad story with a romance and dedicated it to Abraham Lincoln for his forethought in subsidizing railroads. To produce the entertaining and educational epic, William Fox's company hired an army regiment, three thousand railroad workers, a thousand Chinese extras, and more than eight hundred Indian extras and set it in director John Ford's favorite location, Monument Valley.[9]

Roy Stewart starred in *Buffalo Bill on the U.P. Trail* in 1926. True to history, he joins a man named William Rose to build a town on the Union Pacific railroad route through Kansas, but surveyor Roy Webb thwarts his plan, crossing the route through Cody's friend Gordon Kent's property. Cody sides with Kent against the surveyors. Meanwhile, angry at the proposed railroad, Indians start a buffalo stampede. Cody diverts the charge, assists a wounded Indian, and saves Kent's fiancée in the process.[10]

Columbia made the 1954 serial *Riding with Buffalo Bill* starring Marshall Reed in which an outlaw gang led by King Carney also opposes railroad expansion. Their attack on a miner prompts him to ask Cody to disguise himself as the legendary masked man known as "The Ridin' Terror."[11] Continuing the railroad theme, the story line of a "well-plotted, suspenseful western" from Warner Brothers—*Badman's Country* (1958)—involves a gang of outlaws planning to rob a train carrying a half million dollars in gold outside Abilene. Cody (Malcolm Atterbury) joins familiar Old West characters Pat Garrett, Wyatt Earp, Bat Masterson, Harvey Logan, and the Sundance Kid. Garrett, as Abilene's sheriff, hopes to entice the outlaws into town so they can be captured. His fellow lawmen agree to the plan, but the townspeople don't want the rowdies and inevitable gunplay in their town. Eventually they realize that it is the only way they will be free from outlaw threats.[12]

Universal returned with *The Raiders* (1964), James McMullan playing Cody. After the Civil War, Texans driving cattle to Kansas get ambushed when they try to convince railroad men to build into Texas. Cody, Hickok, and Calamity Jane can be found in the plot but, according to one critic, "they add nothing and serve as not much more than comic relief."[13]

Several filmmakers harvested plotlines from Cody's *The Great West That Was* written for Hearst's magazine. In 1926, Ray Taylor directed Edmund Cobb as Cody in *Fighting with Buffalo Bill* for Universal Studios. In it, a father-and-son team of unscrupulous lawyers are traveling with the father's female ward and her boyfriend in a wagon train. The young lady believes her father is dead; the elder lawyer perpetuates the deceit by hiding her father's letters, one of which describes the location of a gold mine. The lawyer plans to reach it before the girl's father returns. Cody's role is to help the girl remain faithful to her boyfriend instead of feeling obliged to accept the advances of the younger lawyer.[14]

Henry McRae, in directing *The Indians Are Coming* for Universal in 1930, adapted another of Cody's stories involving gold, a wagon train, young lovers, Indians, and kidnapping. In the telling, McRae worked out many sound problems long associated with outdoor serials. Starring cowboy actor Tim McCoy, who was a fan of Cody, the film netted nearly $850,000. Will Hays, hired to improve the public image of Hollywood movies, thanked Carl Laemmle for the film, which "brought 20,000,000 children back to the theater."[15]

Battling with Buffalo Bill (1931), one of many films dealing with claim jumpers, was also Cody-inspired and became a thriller for juvenile audiences. Before awarding Tom Tyler the lead, Universal considered Tim McCoy and Johnny Mack Brown. Throughout the series, Cody fights Jim Rodney, Rodney's half-breed henchmen, and Blackfeet. Besides Tyler, who was costumed in Cody's classic buckskins, long hair, and goatee, the producers hired several other silent film stars, including Yakima Canutt.[16]

In some pictures, Cody's role was secondary to that of another Wild West sharpshooter. George Stevens directed Barbara Stanwyck in the title role of the biopic *Annie Oakley* (1935) wherein young Annie, a crack shot, challenges New York sharpshooter Toby Walker to a contest. She purposely loses, but Cody's partner Jeff Hogarth suggests that she join the Wild West show. Moroni Olsen as Buffalo Bill is reluctant to hire her until he sees her shoot. Her talent also impresses Sitting Bull, who calls her "Little Miss Sure Shot" and is responsible for getting Annie and Toby together. A sham rivalry and secret romance between Annie and Toby become a publicity ruse amid Wild West show pageantry. Chief Thunderbird as Sitting Bull has several comedic scenes involving a Murphy bed and gaslights.[17]

Fifteen years later, Irving Berlin's melodies turned the story into the musical *Annie Get Your Gun.* It is surprising that the film, an Academy Award winner for best musical direction and a nominee in other categories, was produced at all. When Metro-Goldwyn-Mayer suspended star Judy Garland for failing to appear on the set, Betty Hutton took over as Annie. Additional problems, including an expense overrun, occurred when the studio refilmed Garland's scenes. Then, Frank Morgan, who was playing Cody, died, necessitating a scramble to locate another actor; Louis Calhern assumed the role.

The story: When the Wild West show comes to Cincinnati, Annie wins a sharpshooting contest over rival Frank Butler and falls in love with him. The show is in financial difficulties, so Cody gives the popular Annie the top spot. Feeling inferior, Frank leaves Cody to join competitor Pawnee Bill. Annie meets Sitting Bull, who persuades her to compete in another match against Frank and to lose in order to get Frank back. When she does, Frank is happy and proposes marriage, an ending that maligns both the real Annie, who was quite self-confident, and Frank Butler, who generously accommodated his wife's fame. Critics found the film "a barrel of fun" and the "happiest thing that has happened to [M-G-M] professionally in a long time."[18]

American Indians were as much a part of the real Buffalo Bill's biography as Annie. Tom Mix and his horse Tony, Jr., starred in *The Miracle Rider* in 1935. Earl Dwire has only a brief moment as Cody early in the film. The western/science fiction serial dealt with the villainous Zaroff, who discovers a highly explosive mineral on Indian land. A scientist in his company devises a remote-controlled glider to frighten the Indians away, but Mix, as Ranger Tom Morgan, uncovers the scheme and saves the reservation.[19]

Richard Arlen played Cody in Screen Guild's 1947 *Buffalo Bill Rides Again.* When oil is discovered on settlers' land, villainous J. B. Jordon instigates an Indian war in an attempt to run off the settlers. When the army sends in Cody to stop the Indians, Jordon's hirelings plot to kill him, but he anticipates the trap they've set. *Variety* found the film, originally titled *Return of Buffalo Bill,* overlong and "short on action." Cliché-ridden dialogue, "actionless" direction, and stilted acting made for seventy minutes of tedium.[20]

A similar story line—*Buffalo Bill in Tomahawk Territory* (1952)— brought Clayton Moore, television's Lone Ranger, to the screen as Cody. He and his sidekick Cactus protect his Indian friends from villains who discover gold on Indian land. A compromise fails when Indian impersonators attack settlers and incite the real Sioux to war. Producers of this "low-budget quickie," first titled *Buffalo Bill's Wagon Train,* used excess stock footage from Ince's early films, dooming it to Saturday afternoon kiddie fare.[21]

Cody having taken his Wild West show abroad for years at a time led to a European familiarity nearly as comprehensive as that of American. As a result, foreign filmmakers found in him an equally fascinating subject. *El Sobrino de don Buffalo Bill* (Buffalo Bill's Nephew) (1944) was a Spanish-made picture. In 1949, Giuseppe Accatino filmed *Buffalo Bill à Roma* for an Italian production company. In 1964 a Cody character turned up in other European films, such as *Sette Ore di Fuoco* (Seven Hours of Gunfire), also known as *Aventuras del Oeste* (Adventures of the West). Joaquin Luis Romero Marchent, one of the first Europeans to make westerns, wrote and directed the film with Rik Van Nutter in the title role. President Grant orders Wild Bill Hickok, Calamity Jane, and Cody—"the figure of a glorious hero"—to learn who is selling arms to the Indians and to stop the warfare. Yellow Hair again appears as Cody's nemesis. Gordon Scott is Cody in *Buffalo Bill, L'Eroe del Far West* (Buffalo Bill, Hero of the Far West), in which he intercedes with Indians and whites for peaceful coexistence. Critic William Judson called the latter "a ridiculous parody."[22] Finally, the 1974 farcical French/Italian production *Touche Pas a la Femme Blanche* (Don't Touch the White Woman), with Catherine Deneuve, starred Michel Piccoli as Cody. The all-star cast also included Marcello Mastroianni as George Custer and Alain Cuny as Sitting Bull. The film reenacts Custer's last stand, most of which takes place on the site of a demolished Parisian mall, an artistic spoof with little regard for history.[23]

Proposing to add to the myriad productions with a Cody character, some filmmakers suggested pictures that were never produced. As early as 1925, former army chief of staff Maj. Gen. Hugh Scott announced a Buffalo Bill movie suggested by the late Gen. Nelson Miles and based on *The Last of the Great Scouts*, a biography by Buffalo Bill's sister Helen Cody Wetmore. Several military men associated with Cody in various campaigns plotted the picture at the fiftieth anniversary of the 1875 West Point class, but it was never made.[24] In 1939, Paramount anticipated a new Buffalo Bill "super-western" costing $1 million. Harry Sherman, producer of *Hopalong Cassidy*, purchased two stories from Frank Winch titled "Pahaska, or the Life of Buffalo Bill" and "Buffalo Bill Frontiersman," with the intention of shooting on location in Big Horn country. James Ellison, who portrayed Cody in *The Plainsman*, was to reprise his role, but this project, too, never got off the ground. Thirty years later, *Cowboys and Indians: The Romantic Life of Buffalo Bill*, with Cary Grant, was scheduled for June 1967 but was not filmed.[25]

The following three films, however, became classics in Cody filmography. During 1936, Cecil B. DeMille cast his new epic, *The Plainsman*, initially titled *Buffalo Bill* (even though Hickok was the hero). For his pictures, DeMille had "no conscience" when it came to rewriting history, which made them "such good fun," wrote one critic. Even before cameras rolled, DeMille anticipated complaints about the film's inaccuracies, but he concluded, "The picture will be history to those who look for that . . . and a western to those who don't."[26]

The plot, based on a Ryley Cooper story and Frank Wilstach's biography *Wild Bill Hickok*, starred Gary Cooper as Hickok, Jean Arthur as a glamorous Calamity Jane, and James Ellison as Cody. It opens around 1864 with newlywed Cody guiding an ammunition shipment through Indian country. Hickok, meanwhile, tries to figure out what Yellow Hand is up to when John Lattimer arrives to sell rifles to the Indians. Cheyennes kidnap Jane and capture Hickok when he attempts to rescue her. To save Hickok from burning at the stake, Jane reveals the army's location. Released, Hickok finds Lattimer in Deadwood and draws on him but instead kills three soldiers. For this he is exiled with a bounty on his head until Custer sends Cody to find him. Meanwhile Sitting Bull defeats Custer in battle and plans to kill more white men using Lattimer-supplied rifles.[27]

"It's pretty much a case of mistaken identities all around," decided a *New York Times* critic. He wondered why DeMille, after tossing so many facts out the window, kept the assassination of Hickok, particularly when studio executives wanted Hickok to survive at film's end. *Motion Picture Herald* summed it up as "quality thrill and action entertainment." Universal Pictures' 1966 remake with Guy Stockwell as Cody drew on the same plot but lacked DeMille's inimitability.[28]

Another classic biopic, a 1944 Twentieth Century-Fox production, was simply titled *Buffalo Bill.* More than five thousand extras including three Indian tribes, twelve hundred buffalo, and three thousand horses appeared in the Technicolor epic along with Joel McCrea as Cody, Maureen O'Hara as Mrs. Cody, Thomas Mitchell as Ned Buntline, and Anthony Quinn as Yellow Hand. A Montana Crow reservation and a specially constructed $60,000 fort provided location scenes.[29]

Wayne Sarf tells the story of director William Wellman who, with Gene Fowler, decided to write a screenplay about the "fakiest guy who ever lived." After the two had butchered Cody on paper, they decided, "you can't stab Babe Ruth, you couldn't kill Dempsey, you can't kill any of these wonderful heroes. . . . Buffalo Bill is a great figure and we cannot do it," so they burned three months' work and started over.[30] Still, Wellman took innumerable liberties with Cody's biography: Cody met his wife Louisa, not a senator's daughter as portrayed, in St. Louis, not in the West as the film claims. His son, who did not die of diphtheria, was not his firstborn. Yellow Hand was not the son of Tall Bull, and Cody killed him by rifle shot, not drowning, at Warbonnet Creek, not War Bonnet Gorge. Even the opening narration— "In 1877, a young man rode out of the West and overnight his name became a household word . . . Buffalo Bill"—is not entirely accurate. Cody was already well known when he starred in his first melodrama in December 1872. The public knew him from numerous dime novels that bore his name and told his exploits. Wellman does offer tension galore, from Indian/cavalry battles to Cody's vacillations over whether to remain in the West or head east toward civilization.[31]

McCrea's Cody is a friend and defender of Indians. When Mr. Frederici, Louisa's father, would solve the Indian "problem" by exterminating them, Cody argues, "Indians are good people if you leave them alone." He accuses Washington's monied interests of instigating Indian wars, saying, "I don't hold with General Sherman that a good Indian is a dead Indian. From what I've seen, the Indian is a free-born American who'll fight for his folks, for his land and for his living . . . just like any other American." McCrea wears Cody's recognizable buckskin outfit, and Quinn is authentically outfitted in correct Cheyenne headgear. The rest of the Indians, however, are "overdressed," an offense typical of Hollywood costuming. The last five minutes of the ninety-minute film encompass Cody's entire Wild West show career, ending with his final farewell.[32]

Mirroring the 1922 court battle over Cody's name, the American Film Institute reported that Twentieth Century–Fox owned several letters from the Cody family protesting the "grossly inaccurate" depiction and complaining that it was made without their permission. The studio claimed that "because Cody was dead, they did not have to obtain the rights to his life story from any of his surviving relatives."[33]

Robert Altman, director of the last in the trio of Cody classics, gave a new generation *Buffalo Bill and the Indians, or Sitting Bull's History Lesson* (1976). In this derisive debunking of Cody's legend, Paul Newman interpreted Cody as "the First Star. He was like one of those people in motion pictures who simply cannot live up to their legends. Their legends are created for them. They are simply human beings. Flawed." Based on his reading of history, Altman, notorious for deflating heroes, portrayed Cody as an "egomaniacal fraud surrounded by other phonies" in action coinciding with Sitting Bull's travels with the Wild West show. Focusing on the dichotomy of reality versus perception, the Buffalo Bill of the public arena—a brave, considerate, and handsome man—is, behind the scenes, prejudiced, drunk, unfaithful, and balding. On the other hand, Sitting Bull is one character who remains true to himself by refusing to participate in the sham reenactments. Comparing America in Cody's time to the 1976 post-Watergate Vietnam era, Altman, by loosely basing his film on Arthur Kopit's drama *Indians*, uses American Indians to represent innocent victims of war.[34]

In a film such as Altman's, the figure of Cody monopolizes nearly every scene. Some filmmakers included a character named Cody only because the film's subject was frontier history. However, *Days of Buffalo Bill* (1946), whose title strongly insinuates that he will be represented, contains no Cody character in the plot at all!

With the advent of television by 1949, westerns once again reigned supreme when scriptwriters mined the Old West for plots as they had for films. Besides expounding on the legends of Wyatt Earp, Annie Oakley, various outlaws, lawmen, and gunmen, they repeatedly reinterpreted Buffalo Bill for the small screen.

In 1974, Roy Huggins satirized the legends of both Cody and Wild Bill Hickok. The script of *This Is the West That Was* called for Cody (Matt Clark), an inept wannabe gunfighter, to envy Hickok's pistoleer reputation. Said reputation, enhanced by Calamity Jane's fawning, leads to a showdown on the streets of Deadwood. Huggins contorts the trio in this comedic treatment that became a cult film on college campuses.[35]

The Young Riders, a 1989 series, stands out as a revelatory take on a teenage Cody when producer Tony Palermo revisited the Pony Express theme with Stephen Baldwin as Cody. Headquartered at a Kansas way station, the riders become involved in adventures occurring in the pre–Civil War years, few of which involved actually riding with the mail. The show lasted nearly two years longer than the mail system on which it was based.

In 1977, Mark Twain and his feuding neighbor Mike Fink briefly encounter Buffalo Bill in the *Incredible Rocky Mountain*

Race when officials of St. Louis, Missouri, sponsor a treasure hunt to the Pacific Ocean. Two years later, in *Last Ride of the Dalton Gang,* Buff Brady makes a fleeting appearance as Cody, and R. L. Tolbert does the same in *Legend of the Golden Gun,* also in 1979. Kenny Rogers as the Gambler in *Gambler III: The Legend Continues* (1987), along with Bruce Boxleitner as Billy Montana, help the Sioux in their fight for government supplies. The two encounter Cody when they uncover corruption at the Indian agency. In another television series, the 1994 *Lonesome Dove,* two of the characters attend the Wild West show.[36] Cody's arena show is also featured in *Hidalgo* (2004), a Touchstone picture allegedly based on the life of Frank Hopkins, a rider with the Wild West. The drama tells the story of Frank and his horse Hidalgo's ride of endurance across the Arabian desert.

The producers of these films illustrated dramatic, convoluted, sometimes silly, and occasionally truly inspired aspects of Cody's military and entertainment careers that nonetheless reinforced his importance in American history. Early in his lifetime, pioneers had ventured into the unmapped frontier, confident they were fulfilling a manifest destiny. Subdued by numerous wars with the U.S. Army, American Indians who once roamed freely over the plains now lived on reservations. More than any other historical re-creation, Cody's Wild West show captured the spirit of the era's legendary people. For easterners and Europeans, he was there to inform and educate. His own life, re-created in arena displays and on film, personified the fortitude, camaraderie, and guts it took to civilize the West.

The mysterious Indian culture fascinated audiences and complemented the historicity of his show. Cody could vouch for the veracity of news reports that focused on frontier peril and the unrelenting potential for conflict, but ultimately his friendly interactions with Indians helped ameliorate white/Indian relations.

Supporters and critics alike commented on his employment of
Indians, but no one could deny he was advancing the government's goal of self-sufficiency for them.

Because viewers' background, education, and prejudices affect
their subjective appreciation, even today any one historical event
offers numerous legitimate interpretations. After film companies
for years recorded Wild West show scenes, Cody's reenactment
of Indian wars in an original moving picture incurred alternate
outbursts of praise and condemnation. The completed movie
showed the army in a victorious light and looked real enough
to military officers who had been present on the field. Con-
versely, Indians perceived the film as a manipulation of the truth.
Regardless of the disparate assertions, Cody and the Essanay
Company brought extraordinary historical validity to the project
with the participation of officers, scouts, and Indians from the
original battles. Few historical films can lay similar claim. The
film's current status as missing, whether caused by man, time,
or nature of the material, continues to frustrate historians and
film enthusiasts.

Then again, our awareness of William Frederick Cody's actual
role in frontier history—whether in dime novels, history books,
film, or television—fulfills his ambition for a long-lasting legacy
after all.

The Film and Television Appearances of William F. "Buffalo Bill" Cody

ABBREVIATIONS: *prod.*= production company; *dir.*= director; *wr.*= story writer; *sp.*= screenplay writer; *Cody* = Cody character played by.

1894: *Seven Acts of Wild West Show; prod.* Edison

1896: *La Cirque Buffalo Bill: Peaux Rouges; prod.* Lumière

1897: *Buffalo Bill and Escort; prod.* Edison

1898: *Parade of Buffalo Bill's Wild West Show; prod.* Edison

1900: *Buffalo Bill's Wild West; prod.* American Mutoscope and Biograph

1900: *Buffalo Bill's Wild West Parade; prod.* American Mutoscope and Biograph

1902: *Buffalo Bill's Wild West Show; prod.* Lubin

1902: *Buffalo Bill's Street Parade; prod.* Lubin

1903: *Buffalo Bill's Parade; prod.* Selig Polyscope

1909: *Les Adventures de Buffalo Bill; dir.* Joe Hamman; *Cody* Joe Hamman

1910: *Life of Buffalo Bill; prod.* Harry Davis and John P. Harris, Buffalo Bill and Pawnee Bill Film; *dir.* Paul Panzer; *wr.* William Wallace Cook

1910: *Buffalo Bill's Far West and Pawnee Bill's Far East; prod.* Buffalo Bill and Pawnee Bill Film; *dir.* Pliny Craft, Johnny Baker

1912: *Life of Buffalo Bill; prod.* Buffalo Bill and Pawnee Bill Film; *dir.* John O'Brien

1913: *The Indian Wars; prod.* Col. Wm. F. Cody Historical Pictures/Essanay; *dir.* Theodore Wharton; *sp.* Charles King

1915: *Patsy of the Circus; prod.* Bison, Universal Pictures; *dir.* Henry MacRae

1917: *The Adventures of Buffalo Bill; prod.* Essanay

1922: *In the Days of Buffalo Bill; prod.* Universal Pictures *dir.* Edward Laemmle; *wr.* Robert Dillon; *Cody* Duke R. Lee

1924: *The Iron Horse; prod.* Fox Film; *dir.* John Ford; *wr.* Charles Kenyon, John Russell; *sp.* Charles Kenyon; *Cody* George Waggner

1925: *The Pony Express; prod.* Famous Players–Lasky; *dir.* James Cruze; *wr.* Henry J. Forman, Walter Woods; *sp.* Walter Woods; *Cody* John Fox, Jr.

1926: *The Last Frontier; prod.* Metropolitan Picture; *dir.* George B. Seitz; *wr.* C. Ryley Cooper; *sp.* William Ritchey; *Cody* Jack Hoxie

1926: *Fighting with Buffalo Bill; prod.* Universal Pictures; *dir.* Ray Taylor; *wr.* Cody's *The Great West That Was; Cody* Edmund Cobb

1926: *Buffalo Bill on the U.P. Trail; prod.* Sunset Productions; *dir.* Frank S. Mattison; *Cody* Roy Stewart

1927: *Buffalo Bill's Last Fight; prod.* MGM; *dir.* John W. Noble; *wr.* Russell Hickson; *Cody* Duke R. Lee

1928: *Wyoming; prod.* MGM; *dir.* W. S. Van Dyke; *wr.* Madeleine Ruthven, Ross Wills; *Cody* William Fairbanks

1931: *Battling with Buffalo Bill;* *prod.* Universal Pictures; *dir.* Ray Taylor; *wr.* Cody's *Great West That Was,* Henry MacRae; *sp.* George Plympton, Ella O'Neill; *Cody* Tom Tyler

1935: *The Miracle Rider;* *prod.* Mascot Pictures; *dir.* Armand Schaefer, B. Reeves Eason; *wr.* Barney Sarecky, Wellyn Totman, Gerald Geraghty; *Cody* Tex Cooper

1935: *The World Changes;* *prod.* First National Film; *dir.* Mervyn LeRoy; *wr.* Sheridan Gibney; *sp.* Edward Chodorov; *Cody* Douglass Dembrille

1935: *Annie Oakley; prod.* RKO Radio Pictures; *dir.* George Stevens; *wr.* Joseph Fields, Ewart Adamson; *sp.* Joel Sayre, John Twist; *Cody* Moroni Olsen

1936: *Custer's Last Stand;* *prod.* Weiss Productions; *dir.* Elmer Clifton; *sp.* George A. Durlam, Eddy Graneman, Bob Lively; *Cody* Ted Adams

1936: *The Plainsman;* *prod.* Paramount Pictures; *dir.* Cecil B. DeMille; *wr.* C. Ryley Cooper, Grover Jones, Frank Wilstach; *sp.* Waldemar Young, Harold Lamb, Lynn Riggs, Jeanie Macpherson; *Cody* James Ellison

1938: *Outlaw Express;* *prod.* Universal Pictures; *dir.* George Waggner; *wr.* Norton S. Parker; *Cody* Carlyle Moore

1938: *Flaming Frontiers; prod.* Universal Pictures; *dir.* Alan James, Ray Taylor; *wr.* Peter Kyne; *sp.* Wyndham Gittens, George Plympton, Basil Dickey, Paul Perez, Ella O'Neill; *Cody* Jack Rutherford

1940: *Pony Express Days; prod.* Warner Brothers; *dir.* B. Reeves Eason; *wr.* Charles Tetford; *Cody* George Reeves

1940: *Young Buffalo Bill; prod.* Republic Pictures; *dir.* Joseph Kane; *wr.* Norman Houston; *sp.* Harrison Jacobs, Robert Yost, Gerry Geraghty; *Cody* Roy Rogers

1942: *Overland Mail; prod.* Universal Pictures; *dir.* Ford Beebe, John Rawlins; *wr.* Johnston McCulley; *sp.* Paul Huston; *Cody* Bob Baker

1944: *Buffalo Bill; prod.* Twentieth Century–Fox; *dir.* William A. Wellman; *wr.* Frank Winch; *sp.* Aeneas Mackenzie, Clements Ripley, Cecile Kramer; *Cody* Joel McCrea

1944: *El Sobrino de Don Buffalo Bill; prod.* Trébol Films; *dir.* Ramon Barreiro; *wr.* Ramon Barreiro

1946: *Days of Buffalo Bill; prod.* Republic Pictures; *dir.* Thomas Carr; *wr.* William Lively, Doris Schroeder; no Cody

1946: *Buffalo Bill Rides Again; prod.* Jack Schwarz Productions; *dir.* Bernard B. Ray; *wr.* Fran Gilbert, Barney Sarecky; *Cody* Richard Arlen

1949: *Buffalo Bill a Roma; prod.* Societa Italiana Lanci Artistici; *dir.* Giuseppe Accatino; *wr.* Giuseppe Accatino, Gian Bistolfi, Redo Romagnoli; *Cody* Enzo Fiermonte

1949: *Law of the Golden West; prod.* Republic Pictures; *dir.* Philip Ford; *wr.* Norman S. Hall; *Cody* Monte Hale

1950: *Annie Get Your Gun; prod.* MGM; *dir.* George Sidney; *wr.* Irving Berlin, Herbert and Dorothy Fields; *sp.* Sidney Sheldon; *Cody* Louis Calhern

1950: *Cody of the Pony Express; prod.* Columbia Pictures; *dir.* Spencer Gordon Bennet; *wr.* Geo. Plympton, Joseph F. Poland; *sp.* Lewis Clay, Charles Condon, David Matthews; *Cody* Dickie Moore

1950: *King of the Bullwhip; prod.* Western Adventures Productions; *dir.* Ron Ormond; *wr.* Jack Lewis, Ira Webb; *Cody* Tex Cooper

1952: *Buffalo Bill in Tomahawk Territory; prod.* Jack Schwarz Productions; *dir.* Bernard B. Ray; *wr.* Sam Neuman, Nat Tanchuck; *Cody* Clayton Moore

1953: *Pony Express; prod.* Paramount; *dir.* Jerry Hopper; *wr.* Frank Gruber; *sp.* Chas. Marquis Warren; *Cody* Charlton Heston

1954: *Riding with Buffalo Bill; prod.* Columbia; *dir.* Spencer Gordon Bennet; *wr.* George Plympton; *Cody* Marshall Reed

1957: *Annie Get Your Gun; prod.* NBC Television; *dir.* Vincent J. Donehue; *Cody* William O'Neal

1957: *The Return of Buffalo Bill: Circus Boy; prod.* Norbert Productions, ABC; *dir.* Fred Jackman, Jr.; *wr.* Jerome Gottler; *sp.* Victor McLeod; *Cody* Dick Foran

1958: *Death Valley Days: Two-Gun Nan; prod.* Filmaster Productions; *wr.* Ruth Woodman; *Cody* William O'Neal

1958: *Badman's Country; prod.* Warner Brothers; *dir.* Fred F. Sears; *wr.* Orville H. Hampton; *Cody* Malcolm Atterbury

1959: *Buffalo Bill; prod.* New World Production, RCA Victor; *Cody* cartoon graphics

1959: *Death Valley Days: Grand Duke; prod.* Filmaster Productions; *dir.* Bernard L. Kowalski; *Cody* John Lupton

1959: *Colt .45: A Legend of Buffalo Bill; prod.* Warner Brothers, ABC; *dir.* Emory Horger; *wr.* James Barnett; *sp.* Willliam Driskill; *Cody* Britt Lomond

1964: *The Raiders (The Plainsman); prod.* Universal Pictures; *dir.* Herschel Daugherty; *wr.* Gene L. Coon; *Cody* James McMullan

1964: *Buffalo Bill, L'Eroe del Far West* (Buffalo Bill, Hero of the Far West); *prod.* Filmes Cinematografica; *dir.* Mario Costa, aka John W. Fordson; *wr.* Nino Straesa, Luciano Martino; *Cody* Gordon Scott

1965: *Sette Ore di Fuoco* (Seven Hours of Gunfire); *prod.* Centauro Films; *dir.* Joaquin Luis Romero Marchent; *wr.* Jose Hernandez, Joaquin Romero Marchent; *Cody* Rik Van Nutter

1966: *The Plainsman; prod.* Universal Pictures; *dir.* David Lowell Rich; *wr.* Michael Blankfort; *Cody* Guy Stockwell

1967: *Annie Get Your Gun; prod.* NBC Television; *dir.* Clark Jones; *wr.* Dorothy and Herbert Fields; *Cody* Rufus Smith

1973: *Los Tres Superhombres en el Oeste* (Three Supermen of the West); *prod.* Cinesecolo Production; *dir.* Italo Martinenghi; *sp.* Italo Martinenghi, Anthony Blod; *Cody* Jose Canalejas

1974: *Touche pas la Femme Blanche* (Don't Touch the White Woman); *prod.* Mara Films; *dir.* Marco Ferreri; *wr.* Marco Ferreri, Rafael Azcona; *Cody* Michel Piccoli

1974: *This Is the West That Was; prod.* Public Art Films; *dir.* Fielder Cook; *wr.* Sam H. Rolfe; *Cody* Matt Clark

1976: *Buffalo Bill and the Indians or, Sitting Bull's History Lesson; prod.* Dino De Laurentis; *dir.* Robert Altman; *wr.* Arthur Kopit; *sp.* Robert Altman, Alan Rudolph; *Cody* Paul Newman

1977: *Incredible Rocky Mountain Race; prod.* SUNN Classic Pictures, NBC Television; *dir.* James L. Conway; *Cody* John Hansen

1979: *The Legend of the Golden Gun; prod.* Columbia Pictures Television; *dir.* Alan J. Levi; *wr.* James D. Parriott; *Cody* R. L. Tolbert

1979: *The Last Ride of the Dalton Gang; prod.* Dan Curtis Productions; *dir.* Dan Curtis; *wr.* Earl W. Wallace; *Cody* Buff Brady

1981: *The Legend of the Lone Ranger; prod.* Universal Pictures, Tanavision, ITC/Wrather Productions; *dir.* William A. Fraker; *sp.* Ivan Goff, Ben Roberts, Michael Kane, Wm. Roberts; *Cody* Ted Flicker

1983: *Voyages! Buffalo Bill and Annie Oakley Play the Palace; prod.* James D. Parriott Productions, NBC; *dir.* Alan J. Levi; *wr.* Jill Sherman; *Cody* Robert Donner

1983: *Voyagers! Sneak Attack; prod.* Scholastic Productions for NBC TV; *dir.* Paul Stanley; *wr.* Harry Longstreet; *Cody* Ike Eisenmann

1983: *Little House on the Prairie: For the Love of Blanche; prod.* Ed Friendly Productions, NBC; *dir.* Michael Landon; *wr.* Michael Landon; *Cody* Eddie Quillan

1984: *Calamity Jane; prod.* CBS Entertainment; *dir.* James Goldstone; *wr.* Suzanne Clauser; *Cody* Ken Kercheval

1987: *Tall Tales and Legends: Annie Oakley; prod.* Gaylord Production, Showtime; *dir.* Michael Lindsay-Hogg; *wr.* Pamela Pettler; *Cody* Brian Dennehy

1987: *The Gambler: Pt. III: The Legend Continues; prod.* Wild Horses Productions, CBS; *dir.* Dick Lowry; *wr.* Roderick Taylor; *sp.* Roderick Taylor, Jeb Rosebrook; *Cody* Jeffrey Jones

1989–92: *The Young Riders; prod.* MGM, ABC; *dir.* various; *wr.* various; *Cody* Stephen Baldwin

1993: *The Wild West; prod.* Rattlesnake Productions; *dir.* various; *Cody* Brian Keith

1994–95: *Lonesome Dove* (series); *prod.* Motown, Pangaea, Qintex; *dir.* various; *wr.* various; *Cody* Dennis Weaver

1995: *Buffalo Girls; prod.* CBS Entertainment; *dir.* Rod Hardy; *wr.* Larry McMurtry; *sp.* Cynthia Whitcomb; *Cody* Peter Coyote

1995: *Wild Bill; prod.* United Artists; *dir.* Walter Hill; *wr.* Pete Dexter; *sp.* Walter Hill; *Cody* Keith Carradine

2004: *Hidalgo; prod.* Touchstone Pictures; *dir.* Joe Johnston; *wr.* John Fusco; *Cody* J. K. Simmons

2001: *Cody! An Evening with Buffalo Bill; prod.* Caravan West Productions; *dir.* Josh Seat; *wr.* Eric Sorg; *Cody* Peter Sherayko

2009: *Murdoch Mysteries: Mild Mild West; prod.* Shaftesbury Films; *dir.* Paul Fox; *wr.* Derek Schreyer; *Cody* Nicholas Campbell

2013, tentative: *The Hard Ride; prod.* Talmarc Film Productions; *dir.* Thadd Turner; *wr.* Thadd Turner; *Cody* Tim Abell

Notes

INTRODUCTION

1. Based on C. Ryley Cooper's account in *Denver Post*, Oct. 15, 16, 1913.

2. *New York Times*, July 30, 1913.

3. Standing Bear, *My People the Sioux*, 260–61.

4. Program, Wild West 1893, Buffalo Bill Historical Center [hereafter BBHC], MS 6, series VI: A, boxes 1–3.

5. Warren, *Buffalo Bill's America*, 468.

6. Etulain, "Cultural Origins," 22.

7. Kammen, *Mystic Chords of Memory*, 271.

8. Although the Mar. 27, 1915, issue of *Moving Picture World* opposed the abbreviation "movies" for motion pictures, calling it "childish," for simplicity I use that term, as well as "cinema" and "film," interchangeably.

CHAPTER 1

1. Hyams, *Life and Times*, 13.

2. Baldwin, *Edison*, 206; Tate, *Edison's Open Door*, 238.

3. BBHC microfilm roll #2, Wm. F. Cody—France 1889 red book; Jonnes, *Eiffel's Tower*, 195.

4. BBHC microfilm roll #2, Wm. F. Cody—France 1889 red book; *Galignani's Messenger,* Aug. 27, 28, 1889.

5. Jonnes, *Eiffel's Tower,* 229.

6. *New York Times,* Aug. 28, 1889.

7. Jonnes, *Eiffel's Tower,* 134; BBHC microfilm roll #2, Wm. F. Cody—France 1889 red book; *New York Herald,* Aug. 14, 1889; *Illustrated London News,* Sept. 1, 1889; *New York Herald,* Aug. 28, 1889.

8. "Cody's Tribute to Edison," BBHC, http://codyarchive.org/multimedia/wfc.aud00002.html.

9. Brownlow and Kobal, *Hollywood,* 28; Gelb and Caldicott, *Innovate like Edison,* 93.

10. Israel, *Edison,* 297; Baldwin, *Edison,* 220.

11. Larson, *Devil in the White City,* 133; *Washington, D.C., Evening Star,* Oct. 23, 1893.

12. Moses, *Wild West Show,* 8; Program, Wild West 1887, BBHC, MS6, series VI: A, boxes 1–3.

13. *Nickelodeon,* Aug. 1, 1910, 63; Conot, *Thomas A. Edison,* 327.

14. Phillips, *Edison's Kinetoscope,* 27; Conot, *Thomas A. Edison,* 331.

15. Israel, *Edison,* 300.

16. *Moving Picture World,* May 4, 1907, 140; Spurr, "Nickelodeons," 565.

17. Spurr, "Nickelodeons," 566; Edwards, "Menace of the Movies," 176.

18. *Moving Picture World,* Oct. 31, 1908, 336.

19. Patterson, "Nickelodeons," 11.

20. Bluestone, "Changing Cowboy," 333.

21. Abel, *Red Rooster Scare,* 164.

22. Bernstein, *Hollywood on Lake Michigan,* 39.

23. Smith, *Shooting Cowboys,* 61; Bowser, *Transformation,* 151.

24. Simmon, *Invention,* 296n1.

25. *Moving Picture News,* May 3, 1913, 7.

26. *Moving Picture World,* Feb. 17, 1912, 558; Smith, *Shooting Cowboys,* 107; *Motion Picture News,* Nov. 25, 1911, 50.

27. "The Popularity of Western Films," *Bioscope,* Aug. 18, 1910, 4–5.

28. Smith, *Shooting Cowboys,* 5.

29. Friar, *Only Good Indian,* 92.

30. *Moving Picture World,* Aug. 5, 1911, 271.

31. *Motion Picture News,* May 17, 1913, 17; Bowser, *Transformation,* 173.

32. *New York Dramatic Mirror,* Dec. 14, 1910.

33. *New York Times,* June 3, 1914, 12.

34. *Moving Picture World,* Nov. 4, 1911, 398.

35. Tuska, "American Western Cinema," 27.

36. Deloria, "Indians," 52.

37. Kilpatrick, *Celluloid Indians,* 17.

38. Ibid., 18; Price, "Stereotyping," 76.

CHAPTER 2

1. Turner, *Significance of the Frontier,* 227; Lescarboura, *Behind the Motion Picture,* 412.

2. "Electricity at the Wild West Show," *Electrical World,* Sept. 15, 1894, 253; BBHC microfilm roll #2, Wm. F. Cody—Brooklyn season 1894, tan book; BBHC microfilm roll #1, Annie Oakley scrapbook 1893–1895; *Electrical Age,* Sept. 15, 1894; *Electrical Review,* Sept. 12, 1894.

3. BBHC microfilm roll #1, Annie Oakley scrapbook, 1893–1895.

4. *East Orange Gazette,* Sept. 27, 1894; *Orange Chronicle,* Sept. 27, 1894.

5. Musser, *Edison,* 125; Phillips, *Edison's Kinetoscope,* 127.

6. Phillips, *Edison's Kinetoscope,* 104–106; the Motion Picture Academy of Arts and Sciences in Los Angeles houses a copy of this film.

7. Ibid., 186; Edison's "Sioux Ghost Dance" can be viewed online at the American Memory project, http://memory.loc.gov/cgi-bin/query/ r?ammem/papr:@filreq(@field(NUMBER+@band(edmp+4024))+@ field(COLLID+edison)).

8. *New York Herald,* Sept. 25, 1894; Musser, *Edison,* 125–26.

9. BBHC microfilm roll #2; *New York Sun,* Sept. 25, 1894; *East Orange Gazette,* Sept. 27, 1894.

10. Phillips, *Edison's Kinetoscope,* 128; To view the film online, see Internet Archive, www.archive.org/movies/thumbnails php?identifier=SF126.

11. *New York Press,* Sept. 25, 1894.

12. Ibid.; Musser, *Edison,* 125–26.

13. *New York Press,* Sept. 25, 1894; *New York Advertiser,* Sept. 25, 1894.

14. Musser, *Edison,* 135–37, 140–41, 145; The film can be seen at Internet Archive, www.archive.org/details/AnnieOakley.

15. See *American Indians in Silent Film,* compiled by Karen C. Lund, at the Library of Congress website: www.loc.gov/rr/mopic/findaid/ indian1.html.

16. Musser, *Edison,* 296, 442; *Newark* (N.J.) *Evening News,* May 20, 1898.

17. Savada, *American Film Institute Catalog,* 128–29.

18. "Buffalo Bill's Wild West Parade," *American History*, http://memory .loc.gov/cgi-bin/query/r?ammem/papr:@field%28NUMBER+@ band%28lcmp002+m2b31268%29%29.

19. Russell, "Buffalo Bill," 33, 34.

20. Ibid.

21. Wetmore, *Buffalo Bill*, 249.

CHAPTER 3

1. Russell, "Buffalo Bill," 33; BBHC, Buffalo Bill archival film compilation #199b.

2. Russell, "Buffalo Bill," 33.

3. *New York Times*, Feb. 22, 1907; *New York Clipper*, Mar. 9, 1907, misspells the name as Voegillo.

4. Program, Wild West 1907, BBHC, MS 6, series VI: A, boxes 1–3.

5. *Albany* (N.Y.) *Evening Journal*, June 15, 1907.

6. Blackstone, *Business of Being*, 35, 38.

7. Kasson, *Buffalo Bill's Wild West*, 153; Rosa and May, *Buffalo Bill*, 188.

8. Program, Wild West 1907, BBHC, MS 6, series VI: A; Hoxie, *Talking Back*, vii.

9. Dixon, *Vanishing Race*, online from Project Gutenberg at http:// www.gutenberg.org/files/27616/27616-h/27616-h.html; Krupicka, "Cody and Wanamaker," 26, 28.

10. Wanamaker Tribute Portfolio, BBHC, MS 6, series IX, box 31; Krupicka, "Cody and Wanamaker," 28.

11. Simmon, *Invention*, 57–60; Blackstone, *Business of Being*, 49.

12. Bowser, *Transformation*, 157; Radbourne, "Out of the West," 52.

13. Deahl, "History," 152, quoting *Illinois State Journal*, Aug. 6, 1909.

14. Gordon W. Lillie, "Major Gordon W. Lillie's Own Story" (ca. 1937.), 17, in BBHC, Curator's Files, Pawnee Bill Lillie folder.

15. *New York Times*, May 15, 1910.

16. Exhibit Z, Documentation relating to Records of District Courts of the United States, U. S. District Court for the District of Colorado, Civil Case Files (Electronic Records); and "The W. J. [*sic*] Cody ('Buffalo Bill') Historical Pictures Co. vs. The Colonial Amusement Co. et. al."; both in Records of the U.S. Information Agency, RG 21, National Archives and Records Administration [hereafter NARA], Denver, Colo.; Ramsaye, *Million and One*, 517.

17. *Moving Picture World,* June 18, 1910, 1042.

18. Ramsaye, *Million and One,* 517

19. Craft to Wm. Wallace Cook, Philadelphia, June 18, 27, 1910, William Wallace Cook Collection, New York Public Library, Manuscripts and Archives Division, Mss Col 654.

20. Craft to Cook, New York City, Aug. 13, 1910, William Wallace Cook Collection, New York Public Library, Manuscripts and Archives Division, Mss Col 654.

21. *New York Clipper,* Sept. 17, 1910, 771.

22. Craft to Cook, Sept. 16, 23, 1910, William Wallace Cook Collection, New York Public Library, Manuscripts and Archives Division, Mss Col 654.

23. Edwards, *Fiction Factory,* 166–67.

24. *Moving Picture World,* Aug. 20, 1910, 401.

25. Ibid.

26. Anderson, "Role of Western," 20.

27. *Der Kinematograph* (Düsseldorf, Germany), Nov. 2, 1910, in Film Motion Pictures file, Curator's files, Buffalo Bill Museum, BBHC.

28. See entry for *The Life of Buffalo Bill* at IMDb, www.imdb.com/title/tt0174875.

29. Ramsaye, *Million and One,* 518.

30. *Moving Picture World,* Mar. 10, 1917, 1509.

31. Golden, "Little White Lies"; Weltman, *Pearl White.*

32. Second affidavit of Lewis Baker, 2, Records of the U. S Information Agency, RG 21, NARA, Denver, Colo.

33. *Moving Picture World,* July 11, 1914, 272.

34. *Utica* (N.Y.) *Dispatch-Herald,* July 10, 1911; Ramsaye, *Million and One,* 518.

35. BBHC, Buffalo Bill archival film compilation #199b.

36. Program, Wild West 1910, BBHC, MS 6, series VI: A.

37. BBHC, Buffalo Bill archival film compilation #199b. The film is also at the Library of Congress.

38. *Moving Picture World,* Dec. 24, 1910, 1471; *Auburn* (N.Y.) *Citizen,* Nov. 26, 1910.

CHAPTER 4

1. Rosa and May, *Buffalo Bill,* 185.

2. Shirley, *Pawnee Bill,* 199.

3. W. F. Cody to "Pard L. W.," North Yakima, Wash., Sept. 7, 1910, in Blackstone, *Business of Being*, 44.

4. Gordon W. Lillie, "Major Gordon W. Lillie's Own Story" (ca. 1937.), in BBHC, Curator's Files, Pawnee Bill Lillie folder.

5. *New York Times*, Mar. 19, 1911.

6. Exhibits Y and Z, Records of the U. S Information Agency, RG 21, NARA, Denver, Colo.

7. Cody to L.W., Bangor, June 1, 1911, in Blackstone, *Business of Being*, 50–51.

8. Cody to Pard (Getchell), St. Louis, Oct. 5, 1911, in Blackstone, *Business of Being*, 53.

9. *New York Clipper*, Nov. 18, 1911.

10. Kiehn, *Broncho Billy*, 279–80; Smith, *Shooting Cowboys*, 49.

11. *Moving Picture World*, Dec. 14, 1912, 1091.

12. Jack O'Brien to Fred Church, Moberly, Mo., Sept. 26, 1911, letter courtesy of David Kiehn.

13. Keil, *Early American Cinema*, 104, quoting *Moving Picture World*, Nov. 27, 1909, 751.

14. Rennert, *100 Posters*, 9.

15. Judson, "Movies," 71.

16. Custen, *Bio/Pics*, 183; Keil, *Early American Cinema*, 69, 71, 72; Merritt, "Dream Visions," 69, 70.

17. Blackhawk Films' notes at the beginning of the film; Creekmur, "Buffalo Bill Himself," 137–39.

18. Creekmur, "Buffalo Bill Himself," 138.

19. *Moving Picture World*, Dec. 14, 1912, 1091.

20. Unidentified clipping in BBHC, Curator's Files, Film—Motion Pictures folder.

21. Pitts, *Hollywood*, 81; Robinson, *From Peep Show*, 145. A copy of the film is in the Ernst Collection, Motion Picture, Broadcasting and Recorded Sound Division, Library of Congress, FLA 1982.

22. *Moving Picture World*, May 4, 1912.

23. *Moving Picture World*, Jan. 4, 1913; 1910 program by Walter Barnsdale for *The Life of Buffalo Bill*, courtesy of Tony Sapienza.

24. *New York Times*, May 30, 1912; *New York Clipper*, June 8, 1912, 5, makes it 3,000 feet; *Moving Picture World*, June 29, 1912, 1238.

25. *New York Clipper*, July 20, 1912, 18.

26. Cody to Cousin Frank, Elgin, Ill., Aug. 27, 1912, in Blackstone, *Business of Being*, 56.

27. *Kansas City* (Kans.) *World*, Oct. 19, 1896.

CHAPTER 5

1. *Denver Post,* July 23, 1913; Shirley, *Pawnee Bill,* 206.

2. Telegram, Frank Baldwin to Nelson Miles, Denver, Jan. 25, 1913, Frank D. Baldwin Papers, Box 5 (E 36), Huntington Library, San Marino, Calif.

3. Fowler, *Timber Line,* 27, 349.

4. Memoranda of Agreement—Cody to join Sells-Floto, BBHC, MS 6, series I: C, box 1, folder 13; *Denver Post,* Feb. 5, 1913.

5. Russell, *Lives and Legends,* 454.

6. Shirley, *Pawnee Bill,* 207.

7. BBHC, MS 6, series I: C, box 1, legal folder FF11; *Park County Enterprise* (Cody, Wyo.), Feb. 26, 1913.

8. Program, Wild West 1912, BBHC, MS 6, series VI: A.

9. "Brother" to Julia, Jackson, Tenn., June 14, 1913, in Foote, *Letters,* 73–74; *New York Times,* Apr. 23, 1913; *Washington Post,* May 22, 1913.

10. *New York Times,* June 8, 1913; W. F. Cody Collection, series 1, box 1 FF2 19, Western History Dept., Denver Public Library.

11. *Denver Post,* July 23, 1913.

12. *Denver Post,* July 6, 13, 1913.

13. *Denver Post,* July 21, 1913.

14. Fowler, *Timber Line,* 318–19.

15. *Denver Post,* July 29, 1913; BBHC, MS 6, series I: C, box 1, folder 13.

16. *North Platte* (Neb.) *Telegraph,* July 31, 1913; BBHC, MS 6, series I: B.

17. *Kansas City Star,* Aug. 17, 1913.

18. *Mansfield* (Ohio) *News,* July 31, 1913; *Park County Enterprise,* Aug. 13, 1913.

19. Cody to "Friend Freeman," Fargo, N.Dak., May 12, 1914, Special Collections, University of Arizona Libraries, Tucson.

20. Turner, *Significance of the Frontier,* 202, 205–206.

21. Program, Wild West 1909, BBHC, MS 6, series VI: A.

22. *Moving Picture World,* July 10, 1909, 48; *Moving Picture World,* Mar. 18, 1911, 581.

23. Robinson, *From Peep Show,* 151.

24. BBHC microfilm roll #1, Wm. F. Cody scrapbook, *Denver Post,* n.d., "Summit Springs" by Maj. Gen. Charles King.

25. Broome, *Dog Soldier,* 167–72; Brown, *Bury My Heart,* 168.

26. Russell, "My Friend," 17–20.

27. "Many Were the Good Tales Told by and about Gallant Charlie King," *Milwaukee Journal*, Mar. 19, 1933, in BBHC MS62 series I-Q, box 2, folder 5; Russell, *Campaigning with King*, 67.

28. Seton, *Book of Woodcraft*, 14.

29. Miles, "Rounding Up the Red Men," 431.

30. *Watertown* (N.Y.) *Times*, Nov. 22, 1890; Maddra, *Hostiles*, 7.

31. James McLaughlin to T. J. Morgan, Standing Rock Agency, June 18, 1890, Oct. 17, 1890, in Office of Indian Affairs, *Annual report of the commissioner of Indian affairs, for the year 1891* G.P.O., [1891], 328–30, University of Wisconsin Digital Collections, http://digital.library.wisc.edu/1711.dl/History.AnnRep91p1.

32. *Watertown* (N.Y.) *Times*, Nov. 22, 1890; Ostler, *Plains Sioux*, 290–91; Maddra, *Hostiles*, 45.

33. Warren, *Buffalo Bill's America*, 378.

34. *Denver Post*, Mar. 7, 1914.

35. Steinbach, *Long March*, 151; *Poughkeepsie* (N.Y.) *Daily Eagle*, Dec. 5, 1890.

36. Ostler, *Plains Sioux*, 304; Steinbach, *Long March*, 153.

37. Russell, *Lives and Legends*, 366.

38. Ibid., 369; Maddra, *Hostiles*, 131.

39. *New York Times*, Mar. 8, 1891.

CHAPTER 6

1. *Denver Post*, Mar. 9, 1914; "Brother" to "Sister," Springfield, Mo., Aug. 22, 1915, in Foote, *Letters*, 76.

2. *Denver Post*, Mar. 9, 1914; *Park County Enterprise*, Sept. 3, 1913.

3. *Cody* (Wyo.) *Park County Enterprise*, July 30, 1913; *Denver Post*, Aug. 21, 1913.

4. *Park County Enterprise*, Aug. 20, 1913; W. F. Cody to Hon. Lindley W. Garrison, Aug. 28, 1913, BBHC, MS 6, series XII: C, box 8.

5. *Denver Post*, Aug. 25, 1913.

6. Bob Lee, *Rapid City Journal*, June 22, 1969; *Denver Post*, Aug. 25, 1913; *Moving Picture World*, Oct. 12, 1907, 503.

7. Telegram, Brennan to Lane, Pine Ridge, Aug. 27, 1913, BBHC, MS 6, series XII: C, box 8; *Rapid City Daily Journal*, Oct. 22, 1913.

8. Frances Belforde-Wayne for Bonfils and Cody to Hon. Franklin K. Lane, Colorado Springs, Aug. 27, 1913, BBHC MS 6, series XII: C, box 8.

9. Franklin Lane to Mr. Secretary, Washington, Aug. 29, 1913, BBHC, MS 6, series XII: C, box 8.

10. "Essanay Studios," Pyramid Beach, Apr. 2011, http://pyramidbeach .com/2011/04/19/essanay-studios; *Denver Post,* Sept. 11, 1913.

11. Wooster, *Nelson A. Miles,* 257; *Park County Enterprise,* Sept. 17, 1913.

12. *Moving Picture World,* Apr. 18, 1914, 349; *Moving Picture World,* Oct. 25, 1913, 368.

13. Ranson, "Nelson A. Miles," 179–81.

14. W. F. Cody Collection, series 1, box 1 FF2 18, Western History Dept., Denver Public Library.

15. Wooster, *Nelson A. Miles,* 257.

16. Hedren, "Charles King," 246, 248; Anderson, "Friendship," 119, 120.

17. Hedren, "Charles King," 251–52; Anderson, "Friendship," 124–25.

18. Anderson, "General Charles King," 98.

19. Memoranda of Agreement, Records of the U. S Information Agency, RG 21, NARA, Denver, Colo.; Cody to Clarence (Rowley), Cody, Wyo., Sept. 24, 1913, BBHC, http://library.bbhc.org/u?/BBOA, 491.

20. *Denver Post,* Sept. 11, 1913.

21. BBHC, Archival Film #23; *Denver Post,* Sept. 16, 17, 1913; Kensel, *Pahaska Tepee,* 46.

22. *Denver Post,* Sept. 23, 1913; Cody to Clarence (Rowley), Cody, Wyo., Sept. 24, 1913, BBHC, http://library.bbhc.org/u?/BBOA,491.

23. Yost, *Buffalo Bill,* 388.

24. *Park County Enterprise,* Oct. 1, 1913.

25. W. F. Cody to Jake, Chicago, Dec. 23, 1914 [*sic,* 1913], BBHC, MS 6, William F. Cody Correspondence Collection.

26. BBHC, Archival Film #23.

27. Cody to Clarence (Rowley), Cody, Wyo., Oct. 4, 1913, BBHC, http: //library.bbhc.org/cdm4/document.php?CISOROOT=/BBOA& CISOPTR=496&CISOSHOW=495&REC=8.

28. Nelson Miles to John Baker, Washington, D.C., Sept. 30, 1913, Frank D. Baldwin Papers Box 5 (E 36), Huntington Library, San Marino, Calif.; *Denver Post,* Sept. 18, 1913.

29. Anderson, "Friendship," 125–26. How much King was paid is not known, but contemporary scenario writers received about $50 for story ideas (Robinson, *From Peep Show,* 154).

CHAPTER 7

1. *Denver Post,* Oct. 3, 1913.

2. *Moving Picture World,* Oct. 25, 1913, 362.

3. *Moving Picture World*, Oct. 25, 1913, 368.

4. Bowser, *Transformation*, 162, 251; Abel, *Encyclopedia*, 70.

5. Balshofer, *One Reel*, 78–79.

6. Everson, *American Silent Film*, 9; *Martin* (Neb.) *Messenger*, Oct. 15, 1913; Abel, *Encyclopedia*, 65, 92; Bowser, *Transformation*, 249.

7. H. K. Hollenbach to Vance E. Nelson, Curator Fort Robinson Museum, Rehrersburg, Pa., June 30, 1974, and Hollenbach, n.d.n.p., "Recalls His Part in Buffalo Bill's Filming of 'Battle of Wounded Knee,'" both in Nebraska State Historical Society, RG 1755.AM, box 1, series 2–3, folders 3, 5.

8. Anderson, "Friendship," 127.

9. Cody, *Memories*, 306; *Denver Post*, Oct. 31, 1913; Anderson, "Friendship," 127.

10. Belle [Day] to "Nete," Wounded Knee Battlefield, Oct. 9, 1913, letter courtesy of David Kiehn.

11. *Denver Post*, Oct. 9, 1913; *New York Clipper*, Nov. 8, 1913; Lescarboura, *Behind the Motion Picture*, 126.

12. Walsh, *Making of Buffalo Bill*, 345; Buecker, "In the Old Army," 18; H. K. Hollenbach to Vance E. Nelson, Curator Fort Robinson Museum, Rehrersburg, Pa., June 30, 1974, Nebraska State Historical Society, RG 1755.AM, box 1, series 2–3, folders 3, 5.

13. Program, Washington, D.C., Feb. 27, 1914, BBHC, MS 6, series I: C, box 1, folder: Historical Picture Co., 6.

14. Hollenbach, n.d.n.p., Nebraska State Historical Society, RG 1755.AM, box 1, series 2–3, folders 3, 5; Cody, *Memories*, 308.

15. Program, Washington, D.C., Feb. 27, 1914, BBHC, MS 6, series I: C, box 1, folder: Historical Picture Co., 7.

16. *Moving Picture World*, Aug. 24, 1912, 777.

17. Program, Washington, D.C., Feb. 27, 1914, BBHC, MS 6, series I: C, box 1 folder: Historical Picture Co., 6, 7.

18. John R. Brennan to Major McLaughlin, Pine Ridge Agency, Oct. 5, 1913, "Miscellaneous Letters Sent by the Agent or Superintendent of the Pine Ridge Agency," NARA microfilm series M1229, reel 69—vol. 73, 365; *Denver Post*, Oct. 9, 1913. Reporter Ryley Cooper misidentified Rodman Wanamaker as John and James Forsyth as Tony Forsythe.

19. *Gordon* (Neb.) *Independent*, Oct. 24, 1913; *Denver Post*, Oct. 11, 1913.

20. *Denver Post*, Oct. 18, 1913. Another legend says a husband and wife were arguing and came to blows. The husband fell by the creek, injured in the knee; *Des Moines* (Iowa) *Sunday Register*, Dec. 28, 1980.

21. *Denver Post*, Oct. 18, 1913.

22. *Denver Post*, Oct. 19, 1913.

23. *Denver Post*, Oct. 24, 1913.

24. Burke, *Buffalo Bill*, 271; Moses, *Wild West Shows*, 234, calls the conspiracy "pure buncombe."

25. Ryley Cooper to E. C. Shepard, Pine Ridge, Oct. 17, 1913, John R. Brennan Diary and Scrapbook, 1907–15, FB28, South Dakota State Historical Society, Moses; *Wild West Shows*, 232.

26. Bowser, *Transformation*, 260.

27. Coleman, *Voices*, 295–321, quotes from the U. S. Adjutant General, "Reports of the Investigation," and interviews from Wounded Knee survivors.

28. Foley, *Father Francis M. Craft*, 90.

29. Philip Wells to Editor, *Rapid City Daily Journal*, Jan. 10, 1914, John R. Brennan Family Papers, F25, South Dakota State Historical Society, letter courtesy of Andrea Faling; *Denver Post*, Oct. 14, 1913.

30. "Mother" to Ruth, Oct 17, 1913, John R. Brennan Family Papers, F25, South Dakota State Historical Society, letter courtesy of Andrea Faling.

31. *Denver Post*, Oct. 14, 1913.

32. *Moving Picture World*, Mar. 14, 1914, 1370; *Denver Post*, Oct. 14, 1913.

33. *New York Times*, Jan. 5, 1891.

34. *Army and Navy Journal*, Nov. 8, 1913, 306–307.

35. *Denver Post*, Oct. 17, 1913.

36. *Denver Post*, Oct. 15, 1913.

37. *Denver Post*, Oct. 20, 1913; Brownlow, *War*, 230.

38. Bob Lee, *Rapid City Journal*, July 6, 1969; *Denver Post*, Oct. 22, 1913.

39. *Denver Post*, Oct. 21, 22, 1913.

40. *Denver Post*, Oct. 21, 26, 1913.

41. *Denver Post*, Oct. 26, 1913.

42. BBHC MS 6, series I: C, box 1, folder: Historical Picture Co.; *Denver Post*, Oct. 21, 1913.

43. *Denver Post*, Oct. 23, 1913; *Moving Picture World*, Mar. 14, 1914, 1370.

44. Moses, *Wild West Shows*, 238.

45. Anderson, "Friendship," 128.

46. *Moving Picture World*, Nov. 22, 1913, 851; "Miscellaneous Letters Sent by the Agent or Superintendent of the Pine Ridge Agency," NARA, microfilm series M1229, roll 74 vol. 78, 139; *Denver Post*, Oct. 29, 1913.

47. "Miscellaneous Letters Sent by the Agent or Superintendent of the Pine Ridge Agency," NARA, microfilm series M1229, roll 70 vol. 74, 378–799. Cody later told a reporter that the Indians were paid two to five dollars a day, resulting in the film company leaving some $40,000 with the Indians—"a costly proposition." BBHC, MS 6, Microfilm roll #1.

48. *Denver Post,* Nov. 21, 1913.

49. Cody to Clarence (Rowley), Cody, Wyo., Nov. 4, 1913, BBHC, http://library.bbhc.org/cdm4/document.php?CISOROOT=/BBOA&CISOPTR=486&CISOSHOW=485&REC=11.

50. *Denver Post,* Nov. 13, 1913; *Moving Picture World,* Nov. 15, 1913, 722; Nov. 22, 1913, 851.

CHAPTER 8

1. Chaplin, *My Autobiography,* 166; Bernstein, *Hollywood,* 42.

2. *Park County Enterprise,* Mar. 4, 1914; Lescarboura, *Behind the Motion Picture,* 64, 202, 210, 212, 216.

3. Bernstein, *Hollywood,* 42; *Moving Picture World,* Feb. 28, 1914, 1097; *Moving Picture World,* Apr. 18, 1914, 349.

4. Azlant, "Screenwriting," 234.

5. Bob Lee, *Rapid City Journal,* July 13, 1969.

6. Moses, *Wild West Shows,* 244; *Denver Post,* Mar. 9, 1914.

7. Robinson, *From Peep Show,* 173–74; *New York Dramatic Mirror,* Feb. 19, 1913, 15; *Motion Picture News,* Nov. 8, 1913, 10.

8. *Denver Post,* Dec. 25, 1913; *Moving Picture World,* Jan. 3, 1914, 54.

9. W. F. Cody to Jake, Chicago, Dec. 23, 1914 [*sic,* 1913], BBHC, MS 6, William F. Cody Correspondence Collection; Cody to Clarence (Rowley), Cody, Wyo., Nov. 4, 1913, BBHC, http://library.bbhc.org/cdm4/document.php?CISOROOT=/BBOA&CISOPTR=486&CISOSHOW=485&REC=11.

10. Anderson, "General Charles King," 94, 96; *Denver Post,* Nov. 11, 1913.

11. *Army and Navy Journal,* Nov. 8, 1913, 306–307.

12. *Lawton* (Okla.) *Daily News,* Jan. 11, 1914, BBHC, MS 6, Box 1, Folder 25.

13. *Chicago Examiner,* Jan. 22, 1914, BBHC, MS 6, Microfilm roll #1.

14. The following scene descriptions taken from Program, Tabor Opera House, Denver, BBHC, MS 62, series I: D, box 3, folder 6. "Black-and-white"

films of the era were not truly black and white. Not only the prairie pictured but entire early films were dun colored.

15. *Denver Post,* Mar. 6, 1914.

16. Ibid.

17. Pony Bob Haslam's Scrapbook, 72.0149, n.p., Jan. 22, 1914, Buffalo Bill Museum, Golden, Colo.; and BBHC, MS 6 Microfilm roll #1 n.d. n.p.

18. BBHC, MS 6 Microfilm roll #1 n.d. n.p.

19. *Denver Post,* Mar. 6, 1914.

20. Munsterberg, *Film,* 19, 47; Thompson, "Movie Violence," 21; *Washington Herald,* Feb. 28, 1914.

21. Nelson Miles to George E. [*sic*] Spoor, Washington, D.C., Jan. 24, 1914, Frank D. Baldwin Papers, Box 5 (E 36), Huntington Library, San Marino, Calif.

22. Nelson Miles to "My Dear General," Boston, Jan. 26, 1914, Frank D. Baldwin Papers, Box 5 (E 36), Huntington Library, San Marino, Calif.

23. Telegram, Cody to Frank Baldwin, Chicago, Jan. 29, 1914, Frank D. Baldwin Papers, Box 5 (E 36), Huntington Library, San Marino, Calif.

24. BBHC, MS 6, microfilm roll #1.

25. *Moving Picture World,* Feb. 8, 1908, 93; *Moving Picture World,* May 16, 1908, 431.

26. *Park County Enterprise,* Feb. 4, 14, 1914; *Moving Picture World,* Feb. 21, 1914, 935.

27. *Washington Post,* Feb. 27,1914.

28. *Denver Post,* Feb. 28, 1914.

29. Ibid.

30. Program for Washington, Feb. 27, 1914, BBHC, MS 6, series I: C, box 1, folder: Historical Picture Co.

31. *Washington Herald,* Feb. 28, 1914.

32. W. F. Cody to "My dear General," Washington, D.C., Feb. 28, 1914, Frank D. Baldwin Papers, box 5 (E 36), Huntington Library, San Marino, Calif.

33. Baldwin to "My dear Colonel," Washington, D.C., Mar. 9, 1914, Frank D. Baldwin Papers, Box 5 (E 36), Huntington Library, San Marino, Calif.

34. *Moving Picture World,* Dec. 13, 1913, 1261; *Moving Picture World,* Feb. 7, 1914, 685; *Moving Picture World,* Mar. 7, 1914.

35. *Moving Picture World,* Dec. 27, 1913, 1521.

CHAPTER 9

1. Governor" to "Tait" (Cody to John H. Tait), Washington, D.C., Feb. 23, 1914, in MS 231 (scrapbook 2), BBHC; Cody to Clarence (Rowley), Cody, Wyo., Oct. 4, 1913, BBHC, http://library.bbhc.org/cdm/compoundobject/collection/BBOA/id/496/show/495; *Denver Post*, Mar. 9, 1914.

2. The phrase refers to a passage in Alexander Pope's "Essay on Man": "Lo! The poor Indian, whose untutored mind sees God in clouds."

3. *Denver Post*, Mar. 7, 1914.

4. *Denver Post*, Mar. 6, 1914.

5. Butsch, *Making of American Audiences*, 152–53.

6. *Rocky Mountain News and Times*, Mar. 8, 1914.

7. *Denver Post*, Mar. 12, 1914.

8. *Denver Post*, Mar. 9, 1914.

9. Ibid.

10. Ibid.

11. *Denver Post*, Mar. 12, 1914; *Omaha Evening Bee*, Mar. 13, 1914.

12. *Park County Enterprise*, Mar. 11, 14, 1914.

13. Ibid.

14. Paul H. Davis, "Investing in the Movies," *Photoplay Magazine*, Aug. 1915, 56; Robinson, *From Peep Show*, 145.

15. Fred [Garlow] to "Father" [Cody], Omaha, Apr. 5, 1914, BBHC MS 6, Correspondence Collection; a standard one-sheet poster measured about 28 by 42 inches; Rennert, *100 Posters*, 5.

16. F. H. Garlow to John R. Brennan, Omaha, Mar. 30, 1914, BBHC MS 6, box 4, folder 4; *Omaha Daily News*, Mar. 27, 29, 1914. A similar article appeared in the *Telluride* (Colo.) *Daily Journal*, Feb. 7, 1914.

17. NARA, Misc. Letters Sent by the Agents or Superintendents of the Pine Ridge Agency, Vol. 77, p. 427–28 (Roll 73), John R. Brennan to J. H. Garland [*sic*], Pine Ridge, Mar. 31, 1914, letter courtesy of Andrea Faling.

18. *Omaha* (Neb.) *Evening Bee*, Oct. 24, 1913.

19. Moorehead, *American Indian*, 132.

20. NARA, Misc. Letters Sent by the Agents or Superintendents of the Pine Ridge Agency, Vol. 77, p. 427–28 (Roll 73), John R. Brennan to Warren K. Moorehead, Jan. 19, 1914.

21. Bob Lee, *Rapid City Journal*, July 6, 1969.

22. *Omaha* (Neb.) *Daily Bee,* Jan. 7, 1891; Hoxie, *Talking Back,* 118.

23. M.R.G. to C. S. Paine, Pine Ridge, Oct. 17 and 18, 1913, Nebraska State Historical Society, RG14, Director's files, letter courtesy of Andrea Faling.

24. *Lincoln* (Neb.) *Daily Star,* Nov. 3, 1913; Gilmore to Friend Paine, Pine Ridge, Oct. 29, 1913, Nebraska State Historical Society, RG14, Director's files.

25. Baldwin to Brennan, Dec. 6, 1913, John R. Brennan Papers, scrapbook 1, South Dakota State Historical Society.

26. Miles had sent an article from *New York World;* Brennan to "My dear General," Pine Ridge, Dec. 6, 1913, Robinson Museum, Pine Ridge Diary, Scrapbook No. 1, Brennan-Wrede Collection, letter courtesy of Andrea Faling.

27. *Rapid City Daily Journal,* Jan. 10, 1914.

28. Moses, *Wild West Shows,* 242.

29. BBHC, MS 6, microfilm roll #1 n.d. n.p.; *Omaha World Herald,* Mar. 19, 1914.

30. *Albuquerque Morning Journal,* Mar. 19, 1914, BBHC, MS 6, microfilm roll #1.

31. *New York Dramatic Mirror,* May 13, 1914.

32. *Chadron* (Neb.) *Journal,* Apr. 17, 1914; *Lincoln* (Neb.) *State Journal,* May 17, 1914; *Alliance* (Neb.) *Semi-Weekly Times,* May 15, 1914.

33. *Lincoln* (Neb.) *Daily Star,* May 18, 19, 21, 22, 1914; *Lincoln* (Neb.) *State Journal,* May 22, 1914.

34. *Des Moines Daily News,* May 3, 1914; *Brooklyn* (N.Y.) *Daily Eagle,* May 19, 1914.

35. Anderson, "General Charles King," 94, 95; Anderson, "Friendship," 130–31.

36. *Denver Post,* Mar. 9, 1914; *Moving Picture World,* Sept. 12, 1914.

37. *Decatur Daily Review,* July 14, 1914; *Oelwein* (Iowa) *Daily Register,* July 23, 1914; *Cedar Rapids Republican,* July 29, 1914; *Carroll* (Iowa) *Times,* Aug. 13, 1914.

38. *Park County Enterprise,* Oct. 17, 21, 1914.

39. *Los Angeles Times,* Oct. 11, 1914; *Perry* (Iowa) *Daily Chief,* Nov. 14, 1914; *Lacrosse* (Wisc.) *Tribune,* Dec. 10, 1914; *Fort Wayne Journal Gazette,* Dec. 10, 1914.

40. *Moving Picture World,* Nov. 7, 1914, 813.

41. Affidavit of Louis Levand, 3–4, in NARA, RG 21, Denver, Colo; Hollywood Center Studios, www.robinsonhope.com/hollywoodcenter/history/timeline.html.

42. *Park County Enterprise,* June 23, 1915.

43. Affidavit of Lewis H. Baker, Nov. 4, 1922, 6, 7, in NARA, RG 21, Denver, Colo.

CHAPTER 10

1. Whissel, "Placing the Spectator," 227.

2. Quoted in Carter, *Buffalo Bill Cody,* 454.

3. *Denver Post,* Mar. 9, 1914.

4. Paul H. Davis, "Investing in the Movies," *Photoplay Magazine,* Sept. 1915, 123; Tarbox, *Lost Films,* 111.

5. *Nickelodeon,* Feb. 18, 1911; *Moving Picture World,* Sept. 16, 1911, 733; *Motion Picture News,* Nov. 18, 1911, 22.

6. "Brother" to "My Dear Sister," New Rochelle, Feb. 8, 1916, in Foote, *Letters,* 77.

7. Cody, *Buffalo Bill's Life Story,* 189–90.

8. *Moving Picture World,* Feb. 17, 1912; Smith, *Shooting Cowboys,* 107, 109.

9. BBHC, microfilm roll #1, n.d. n.p.; *New York Dramatic Mirror,* Dec. 3, 1913, 27.

10. Bowser, *Transformation,* 48; Brownlow, *War,* 223.

11. *Motion Picture News,* Nov. 25, 1911.

12. *Moving Picture World,* Oct. 21, 1911, 189; *Moving Picture World,* Jan. 23, 1915, 489; Jacobs, *Rise,* 168, 270–71.

13. Friar, *Only Good Indian,* 93.

14. *New York Dramatic Mirror,* Aug. 20, 1913, 31; *Baldwinsville* (N.Y.) *Gazette and Farmers' Journal,* Jan. 25, 1917.

15. Nasaw, *Going Out,* 206; Fielding, *American Newsreel,* 96.

16. Jacobs, *Rise of the American Film,* 271–72; Brownlow and Kobal, *Hollywood,* 63, 80–81.

17. Friar, *Only Good Indian,* 139, 141.

18. *Moving Picture World,* July 11, 1914, 185; *Moving Picture World,* Jan. 2, 1915, 45; *Motion Picture News,* Sept. 7, 1913, 20.

19. *New York Times,* Apr. 12, 1914; *Moving Picture World,* Nov. 22, 1913.

20. Mintz and Roberts, *Hollywood's America,* 6.

21. May, *End of American Innocence,* 335, 337–38; Fielding, *American Newsreel,* 58.

22. Steiner, *Rise of Urban America,* 62, 65, 70, 83, 116–17; Nasaw, *Going Out,* 96–97.

23. Bob Lee, *Rapid City Journal*, Aug. 3, 1969; Everson, *American Silent Film*, 223.

24. Brownlow, *War*, 228.

25. "Brother" to "Sister," Springfield, Mo., Aug. 22, 1915, in Foote, *Letters*, 76; Walsh, *Making of Buffalo Bill*, 352.

26. "Brother" to "My Dear Sister," New Rochelle, Feb. 8, 1916, in Foote, *Letters*, 77; G. W. Lillie to "My Dear Col.," Pawnee, Okla., June 3, 1916, letter courtesy of Tony Sapienza.

CHAPTER 11

1. BBHC, MS 6, series I: C, box 1, new folder: promotional pamphlets.

2. *Film World and A-V News Magazine* 20, no. 1 (1964), 8, 9; Library of Congress, American Film Institute, Nichol Collection, FAA 2030 by Ford 1917.

3. Mulroy, *Western Amerykanski*, 94–95.

4. Yost, *Buffalo Bill*, 480–81n31; also in December 1913, the Selig Polyscope Company reportedly bought out the remainder of Pawnee Bill's Wild West show for use in its films; *New York Dramatic Mirror*, Dec. 10, 1913, 27.

5. E. J. Ayers to Colonel Cody, Washington, D.C., Dec. 18, 1915; W. F. Cody to Ayers, New Rochelle, Jan. 27, 1916; Memorandum, D. C. to Mr. Ayers, Washington, Jan. 28, 1916; E. J. Ayers to "My dear Colonel Cody," Jan. 29, 1916; W. F. Cody to "Sir," New Rochelle, Feb. 1, 1916; Ayers to "Gentlemen," Essanay Film Co., Washington D.C., Feb. 2, 1916; Ayers to "Gentlemen," Essanay Film Co., Washington, D.C., Mar. 7, 1916, all in BBHC, MS 6, series XII: C, box 8.

6. V. R. Day to E. J. Ayers, Chicago, Mar. 21, 1916; Ayers to "My dear Colonel Cody," Washington, D.C., Mar. 23, 1916, both in BBHC, MS 6, series XII: C, box 8; Walsh, *Making of Buffalo Bill*, 354, also in Burke, *Buffalo Bill*, 281.

7. W. F. Cody to A [*sic*]. J. Ayers, Cody, Wyo., Mar. 31, 1916; Ayers to "My dear Mr. Cody," Washington, D.C., Apr. 6, 1916, both in BBHC, MS 6, series XII: C, box 8.

8. Affidavit of George Spoor, 4, and Supplemental disposition of George Spoor, 2, 3, NARA, RG 21, Denver, Colo. Two years later, when the George Kleine Exchange ceased business, all copies of the film were returned to Essanay, except those stolen in the interim.

9. *Moving Picture World,* Jan. 27, 1917, 553; *Moving Picture World,* Feb. 3, 1917, 672.

10. *Rochester* (N.Y.) *Democrat and Chronicle,* Jan. 28, 29, 1917.

11. Affidavit of Lewis H. Baker, 8, NARA, RG 21, Denver, Colo.

12. *Universal Weekly,* Aug. 26, Sept. 2, Sept. 9, Sept. 30, 1922.

13. Affidavit of Lewis H. Baker, 7, and Memo on motion for injunction, 1, NARA, RG 21, Denver, Colo.; Affidavit of George Spoor, 2, NARA, RG 21, Denver, Co.

14. *Universal Weekly,* Aug. 19, 1922–Jan. 6, 1923.

15. Affidavit of Pliny Craft, 2, and deposition of Willard S. McKay, 3–5, NARA, RG 21, Denver, Colo.

16. Exhibits K-1, K-3, K-4, NARA, RG 21, Denver, Colo.

17. Levand, 5, 12; Exhibit S, NARA, RG 21, Denver, Colo.

18. *Universal Weekly,* Aug. 26, 1922; brief of defendants, 39, NARA, RG 21, Denver, Colo.

19. Brief of plaintiff in reply to brief of defendants, 15, NARA, RG 21, Denver, Colo.

20. Deposition E. H. Goldstein, 1, 2; affidavit of John S. Broughton, 3, NARA, RG 21, Denver, Colo.

21. Affidavit of Eugene Gerbase, NARA, RG 21, Denver, Colo.

22. Brief of defendants, 18–19, NARA, RG 21, Denver, Colo.

23. *Federal Reporter* 284, Dec. 1922–Feb. 1923, 873–77.

24. Russell, "Buffalo Bill," 33.

25. Slide, *Nitrate Won't Wait,* 1, 3, 5.

26. W.B. Acker to Roza I. Odell, Washington, D.C., July 12, 1930, in BBHC, MS6 series IV, box 1, folder 4; Moses, *Wild West Shows,* 245.

27. Bob Lee to Durrett Wagner, editor Swallow Press, Spearfish, June 3, 1978, formerly in the Bob Lee Papers, Leland D. Case Library, Black Hills State University, Spearfish, S.Dak.; personal communication, Roberta Sago, Oct. 22, 2009; Bob Lee, *Rapid City Journal,* July 20, 1969.

28. Personal communication, Paul Fees, Oct. 3, 2009; BBHC, Archival footage #23.

29. Hiram S. Cody to M. O. Steen, Winston-Salem, Oct. 7, 1960, in BBHC, Buffalo Bill Museum, Curator's Files: Film Motion Pictures—Buffalo Bill; Bernstein, *Hollywood,* 37.

30. Grimm, "Paper Print Pre-history," 205.

31. Film Preservation Photo Gallery, National Film Preservation Board, www.loc.gov/film/photogal.html.

32. *Motography* 13, no. 14 (Apr. 3, 1915).

33. Personal communication, David Phillips, June 22, 2008.

34. BBHC, Archival footage #23.

35. BBHC, Buffalo Bill compilation film #199b.

36. Rose, "Lust for the Trail Dust," 23.

CHAPTER 12

1. Gevinson, *American Film Institute Catalog*, 568.

2. Everson, *American Silent Film*, 147; Pitts, *Hollywood*, 234–35.

3. *Variety*, July 20, 1938; Gevinson, *American Film Institute Catalog*, 751–52.

4. Cline, *In the Nick of Time*, 10, 221.

5. *Variety*, Dec 6, 1939; Cline, *In the Nick of Time*, 233. The episode titles were 1, "A Race with Disaster"; 2, "Flaming Havoc!" 3, "The Menacing Herd"; 4, "The Bride of Disaster"; 5, "Hurled to Death"; 6, "Death at the Stake"; 7, "The Path of Peril"; 8, "Imprisoned in Flames"; 9, "Hidden Danger"; 10, "Blazing Wagons"; 11, "The Trail of Terror"; 12, "In the Claws of the Cougar"; 13, "The Frenzied Mob"; 14, "The Toll of Treachery"; 15, "The Mail Goes Through."

6. *New York Times*, July 8, 1949; Lentz, *Western and Frontier Film*, 1084; Cline, *In the Nick of Time*, 40. Episode titles: 1, "Cody Carries the Mail"; 2, "Captured by Indians"; 3, "Cody Saves a Life"; 4, "Cody Follows a Trail"; 5, "Cody to the Rescue"; 6, "The Fatal Arrow"; 7, "Cody Gets His Man"; 8, "Revenge Raiders"; 9, "Frontier Law"; 10, "Cody Tempts Fate"; 11, "Trouble at Silver Gap"; 12, "Cody Comes Through"; 13, "Marshall of Nugget City"; 14, "Unseen Danger"; 15, "Cody's Last Ride."

7. *Los Angeles Times*, May 3, 7, 1953; *New York Times*, June 6, 1953; Andreychuk, *American Frontiersmen*, 196–97; Judson, "Movies," 80; *Variety*, Mar. 4, 1953.

8. Film Motion Pictures—Buffalo Bill, Buffalo Bill Museum Curator's Files, in *AFI*, 1166–67; *Variety*, May 8, 1940.

9. *New York Times*, Aug. 29, 1924; *Los Angeles Times*, Feb. 22, 1925; Pitts, *Hollywood*, 173, 175.

10. Judson, "Movies," 73–74; Gevinson, *American Film Institute Catalog*, 141.

11. Lentz, *Western and Frontier Film*, 1357. Episode titles: 1, "The Ridin' Terror from St. Joe"; 2, "Law of the Six Guns"; 3, "Raiders from Ghost Town"; 4, "Cody to the Rescue"; 5, "Midnight Marauders"; 6, "Under the Avalanche"; 7, "Night Attack"; 8, "Trapped in a Power Shack";

9, "Into an Outlaw Trap"; 10, "Blast to Oblivion"; 11, "The Depths of the Earth"; 12, "The Ridin' Terror"; 13, "Trapped in the Apache Mine"; 14, "Railroad Wreckers"; 15, "Law Comes to the West."

12. *Variety*, May 28, 1958.

13. Garfield, *Western Films*, 263.

14. Lahue, *Continued Next Week*, 251–52; *Los Angeles Times*, Apr. 15, 1926. Episode titles: 1, "Westward"; 2, "The Red Menace"; 3, "The Blazing Arrow"; 4, "The Death Trap"; 5, "The Renegade"; 6, "The Race"; 7, "Buried Alive"; 8, "Desperate chances"; 9, "The Shadow of Evil"; 10, "At the End of the Trail."

15. Lahue, *Continued Next Week*, 151–52; Lentz, *Western and Frontier Film*, 1208–1209. Episode titles: 1, "Pals in Buckskin"; 2, "Call to Arms"; 3, "Furnace of Fear"; 4, "Red Terror"; 5, "Circle of Death"; 6, "Hate's Harvest"; 7, "Hostage of Fear"; 8, "Dagger Duel"; 9, "Blast of Death"; 10, "Redskin's Revenge"; 11, "Frontiers of Flame"; and 12, "Trail's End."

16. *New York Times*, Oct. 10, 1931; Cline, *In the Nick of Time*, 83, 204. Episode titles: 1, "Captured by Redskins"; 2, "Circling Death"; 3, "Between Hostile Tribes"; 4, "The Savage Horde"; 5, "The Fatal Plunge"; 6, "Trapped"; 7, "The Unseen Killer"; 8, "Sentenced to Death"; 9, "The Death Trap"; 10, "Shot from Ambush"; 11, "The Flaming Death"; and 12, "Cheyenne Vengeance."

17. *Los Angeles Times*, July 22, 1935; *New York Times*, Dec. 24, 1935; *Variety*, Dec. 25, 1935.

18. Gevinson, *American Film Institute Catalog*, 39-40; *Los Angeles Times*, May 19, 23, 1949; *Los Angeles Times*, May 25, June 5, 1950; Parish and Pitts, *Great Hollywood*, 15–18; Kay, "You Can Get," 11.

19. Cline, *In the Nick of Time*, 212–13. Episode titles: 1, "The Vanishing Indian"; 2, "The Firebird Strikes"; 3, "The Flying Knife"; 4, "A Race with Death"; 5, "Double Barreled Doom"; 6, "Thundering Hoofs"; 7, "The Dragnet"; 8, "Guerrilla Warfare"; 9, "The Silver Band"; 10, "Signal Fires"; 11, "A Traitor Dies"; 12, "Danger Rides with Death"; 13, "The Secret of X-94"; 14, "Between Two Fires"; 15, "Justice Rides the Plains."

20. Gevinson, *American Film Institute Catalog*, 141; *Variety*, Apr. 2, 1947.

21. *Variety*, Jan. 30, 1952; Gevinson, *American Film Institute Catalog*, 141.

22. Judson, "Movies," 79.

23. *Los Angeles Times*, Sept. 22, 1974.

24. *New York Times*, June 22, 1925; *Los Angeles Times*, June 22, 1925.

25. *Los Angeles Times*, Feb. 15, 1939; *New York Times*, Feb. 15, 1939; *Los Angeles Times*, June 19, 1967.

26. *New York Times*, June 26, 1936; *Los Angeles Times*, Jan. 14, 1937; *Los Angeles Times*, Nov. 24, 1935; *Los Angeles Times*, Jan. 15, 1937.

27. *Los Angeles Times*, Oct. 11, 1935; Vermilye, *Films of the Thirties*, 180–81; *Variety*, Jan. 20, 1937; *Magill's American Film Guide*, 4:2623–25.

28. *New York Times*, Jan. 17, 1937.

29. BBHC, MS 62, series I-D, box 4, folder 20.

30. Sarf, *God Bless You*, 245.

31. Ibid., 245–48; BBHC, MS 62, series I-D, box 4, folder 20.

32. Gagliasso, "Joe De Yong," 13; Gevinson, *American Film Institute Catalog*, 139–40; *Variety*, Mar. 15, 1944.

33. Gevinson, *American Film Institute Catalog*, 139–40.

34. *Oswego* (N.Y.) *Palladium Times*, July 17, 1976; Coyne, *Crowded Prairie*, 169–72; *Variety*, June 30, 1976.

35. Maril, *Movies*, 417.

36. *Los Angeles Times*, Dec. 17, 1977.

Bibliography

Abel, Richard, ed. *Encyclopedia of Early Cinema*. London: Rutledge, 2005.
———. *The Red Rooster Scare: Making Cinema American 1900–1910*. Berkeley: University of California Press, 1999.
Adams, Les, and Buck Rainey. *Shoot-Em-Ups: The Complete Reference Guide to Westerns of the Sound Era*. New Rochelle, N.Y.: Arlington House, 1978.
Aleiss, Angela. "Native Americans: The Surprising Silents." *Cineaste* 21, no. 3 (1995): 34–35.
Allen, Robert C. "From Exhibition to Reception: Reflections on the Audience in Film History." *Screen* 31, no. 4 (1990): 347–56.
American Film Institute Catalog of Motion Pictures Produced in the United States. Berkeley: University of California Press, 1971–.
Anderson, Harry H. "The Friendship of Buffalo Bill and Charles King." *Milwaukee History* 9 (Winter 1986): 119–32.
———. "General Charles King and Buffalo Bill's Silent Western Movies." *Historical Messenger of Milwaukee County Historical Society*, no. 22 (1966): 93–98.
Anderson, Robert. "The Role of Western Film Genre in Industry Competition 1907–1911." *Journal of the University Film Association* 31, no. 2 (1979): 19–26.
Andreychuk, Ed. *American Frontiersmen on Film and Television: Boone, Crockett, Bowie, Houston, Bridger and Carson*. Jefferson, N.Car.: McFarland, 2005.

Azlant, Edward. "Screenwriting for the Early Silent Film: Forgotten Pioneers, 1897–1911." *Film History* 9, no. 3 (1997): 228–56.

Baldwin, Neil. *Edison: Inventing the Century.* New York: Hyperion, 1995.

Balio, Tino, ed. *The American Film Industry.* Madison, Wisc.: University of Wisconsin Press, 1976, 1985.

Balshofer, Fred J. *One Reel a Week.* Berkeley: University of California Press, 1967.

Bataille, Gretchen, and Charles L. P. Silet. "The Entertaining Anachronism: Indians in American Film." In *The Kaleidoscope Lens,* ed. Randall M. Miller. Jerome S. Ozer, 1980.

Bernardi, Daniel, ed. *The Birth of Whiteness: Race and the Emergence of U.S. Cinema.* New Brunswick, N.J.: Rutgers University Press, 1996.

Bernstein, Arnie. *Hollywood on Lake Michigan: 100 Years of Chicago and the Movies.* Chicago: Lake Claremont Press, 1998.

Blackstone, Sarah. *Buckskins, Bullets and Business.* Westport, Conn.: Greenwood Press, 1986.

———. *The Business of Being Buffalo Bill: Selected letters of William F. Cody, 1879–1917.* New York: Praeger, 1988.

Bluestone, George. "The Changing Cowboy: From Dime Novel to Dollar Film." *Western Humanities Review* 14 (Summer 1960): 331–37.

Boatright, Mody. "The Cowboy Enters the Movies." In *The Sunny Slopes of Long Ago,* ed. Wilson M. Hudson and Allen Maxwell. Dallas, Tex.: Southern Methodist University Press, 1966.

Bowser, Eileen. *The Transformation of Cinema 1907–1915.* Berkeley: University of California Press, 1990.

British Film Institute Catalog. London: British Film Institute, 1991.

Broome, Jeff. *Dog Soldier Justice: The Ordeal of Susanna Alderdice in the Kansas Indian War.* Lincoln, Kans.: Lincoln County Historical Society, 2003; reprint, Lincoln: University of Nebraska Press, 2009.

Brown, Dee. *Bury My Heart at Wounded Knee.* New York: Holt, Rinehart and Winston, 1971.

Brownlow, Kevin. *The War, the West and the Wilderness.* New York: Alfred A. Knopf, 1979.

Brownlow, Kevin, and John Kobal. *Hollywood: The Pioneers.* New York: Alfred A. Knopf, 1979.

Buecker, Thomas R., ed. "In the Old Army: Harry K. Hollenbach at Fort Robinson, 1911–1913." *Nebraska History* 71, no. 1 (1990): 13–22.

———. *Fort Robinson and the American Century, 1900–1948.* Norman: University of Oklahoma Press, 2004.

Burg, David F. *Chicago's White City of 1893*. Lexington: University Press of Kentucky, 1976.

Burke, John. *Buffalo Bill, the Noblest Whiteskin*. New York: G. P. Putnam's Sons, 1973.

Buscombe, Edward, ed. *The BFI Companion to the Western*. New York: Atheneum, 1988.

———. *"Injuns!" Native Americans in the Movies*. London: Reaktion Books, 2006.

Butsch, Richard. *The Making of American Audiences: From Stage to Television, 1750–1990*. Cambridge, Mass.: Cambridge University Press, 2000.

Calder, Jenni. *There Must Be a Lone Ranger: The American West in Film and in Reality*. New York: Taplinger, 1975.

Cameron-Wilson, James, and Adam Keen. *Film Review 2004–2005*. London: Reynolds and Hearn, 2004.

Carmichael, Deborah. "The American West(s) in Film, Television, and History." *Film History* 33, no. 1 (2003): 7–9.

Carnes, Mark C., ed. *Past Imperfect: History According to the Movies*. New York: Henry Holt, 1995.

Carstensen, Vernon. "Making Use of the Frontier and the American West." *Western History Quarterly* 13, no. 1 (1982): 5–16.

Carter, Robert A. *Buffalo Bill Cody: The Man behind the Legend*. New York: John Wiley and Sons, 2000.

Cawelti, John G. "Cowboys Indians Outlaws." *American West*, Spring 1964, 29–35, 77–79.

———. *The Six-Gun Mystique*. Bowling Green, Ohio: Bowling Green State University Popular Press, 1984.

Chaplin, Charles. *My Autobiography*. New York: Simon and Schuster, 1964.

Cline, William C. *In the Nick of Time*. Jefferson, N.Car.: McFarland, 1984.

Cocks, Orrin G. "Moving Pictures as a Factor in Municipal Life." *National Municipal Review*, October 14, 1914, 708–12.

Cody, Louisa, with Courtney Ryley Cooper. *Memories of Buffalo Bill*. New York: Appleton, 1919.

Cody, Colonel W. F. *Buffalo Bill's Life Story: An Autobiography*. New York: Farrar and Rinehart, 1920; reprint, Toronto: General Publishing, n.d.

———. *The Life of Buffalo Bill*. Hartford, Conn.: Frank E. Bliss, 1979; reprint, Lincoln: University of Nebraska Press, 1978.

Coleman, William S. E. *Voices of Wounded Knee*. Lincoln: University of Nebraska Press, 2000.

Connelly, Robert B. *The Motion Picture Guide, Silent Film 1910–1936.* Chicago: Cinebrooks, 1986.

Conot, Robert. *Thomas A. Edison: A Streak of Luck.* New York: DaCapo Press, 1979.

Cook, David A. *A History of Narrative Film.* New York: W. W. Norton, 1982.

Coyne, Michael. *The Crowded Prairie: American National Identity in the Hollywood Western.* London: I. B. Tauris, 1998.

Creekmur, Corey K. "Buffalo Bill Himself." In Janet Walker, ed., *Westerns: Films through History.* New York: American Film Institute, 2001.

Currie, Barton W. "The Nickel Madness." *Harper's Weekly,* August 24, 1907, 1246–47.

Custen, George F. *Bio/Pics: How Hollywood Constructed Public History.* New Brunswick, N.J.: Rutgers University Press, 1992.

Deahl, William E., Jr. "A History of Buffalo Bill's Wild West Show, 1883–1913." Unpublished diss., Southern Illinois University, August 1974.

deCordova, Richard. *Picture Personalities: The Emergence of the Star System in America.* Chicago: University of Illinois Press, 1990.

Deloria, Vine, Jr. "The Indians." In Brooklyn Museum, *Buffalo Bill and the Wild West.* Pittsburgh: University of Pittsburgh Press, 1981.

Dixon, Joseph K. *The Vanishing Race.* New York: Doubleday, Page, 1914. www.gutenberg.org/files/27616/27616-h/27616-h.html.

Dunbar, Olivia Howard. "The Lure of the Films." *Harper's Weekly,* January 18, 1913, 20, 22.

Eaton, Walter Prichard. "The Theater: The Menace of the Movies." *American Magazine,* September 1913, 55–60.

Edwards, Harold. "The Menace of the Movies." *Theater Magazine,* October 22, 1915, 176–78.

Edwards, John Milton (aka William Wallace Cook). *The Fiction Factory.* Ridgewood, N.J.: The Editor Company, 1912.

Etulain, Richard W. "Cultural Origins of the Western." In Jack Nachbar, ed. *Focus on the Western.* Englewood Cliffs, N.J.: Prentice-Hall, 1974.

———, ed. *Western Films: A Brief History.* Manhattan, Kans.: Sunflower University Press, 1983.

Everson, William K. *American Silent Film.* New York: Oxford University Press, 1978.

———. *The Hollywood Western: 90 Years of Cowboys and Indians, Train Robbers, Sheriffs and Gunslingers, and Assorted Heroes and Desperados.* New York: Citadel Press, 1969, 1992.

————. *A Pictorial History of the Western Film.* New York: Citadel Press, 1969.

Fenin, George N., and William K. Everson. *The Western: from Silents to the Seventies.* New York: Grossman, 1962, 1973.

Fielding, Raymond. *The American Newsreel 1911–1967.* Norman: University of Oklahoma Press, 1972.

Foley, Thomas W. *Father Francis M. Craft, Missionary to the Sioux.* Lincoln, Neb.: Bison Books, 2007.

Foote, Stella Adelyne. *Letters from Buffalo Bill.* Billings, Mont.: Foote, 1954.

Fordin, Hugh. *The World of Entertainment: Hollywood's Greatest Musicals.* Garden City, N.Y.: Doubleday, 1975.

Forsher, James. *The Community of Cinema.* New York: Praeger, 2003.

Fowler, Gene. *Timber Line.* Sausalito, Calif.: Comstock Editions, 1933.

Francaviglia, Richard, and Jerry Rodnitzky, eds. *Lights, Camera, History: Portraying the Past in Film.* College Station: Texas A&M University Press, 2007.

Freeman, Joseph. "Biographical Films." *Theater Arts Monthly,* December 1941, 900–906.

French, Philip. "The Indian in the Western Movie." *Art in America* 60 (July–August 1972): 32–39.

Friar, Ralph and Natasha. *The Only Good Indian: The Hollywood Gospel.* New York: Drama Book Specialists, 1972.

Frink, Maurice. "Short Bull and the Hungry Hearts, Part II." *Chicago Westerners Brand Book* 27, no. 7 (1970): 49–52.

Gagliasso, Dan. "Joe De Yong and Hollywood." *Montana: The Magazine of Western History* 50, no. 3 (2000): 2–17.

Garfield, Brian. *Western Films.* New York: Rawson, 1982.

Gelb, Michael, and Sarah Miller Caldicott. *Innovate like Edison: The Success System of America's Greatest Inventor.* New York: Dutton, 2007.

Gevinson, Alan, ed. *American Film Institute Catalog. Within Our Gates: Ethnicity in American Feature Films, 1911–1960.* Berkeley: University of California Press, 1997.

Golden, Eve. "Little White Lies: The Elusive Life of Pearl White." *Classic Images* 265 (1997).

Grau, Robert. *The Business Man in the Amusement World.* New York: Broadway, 1910.

Gregory, Carl Louis. "Resurrection of Early Motion Pictures." *Journal of the Society of Motion Picture Engineers* 42, no. 3 (1944): 159–69.

Grimm, Charles "Buckey." "A Paper Print Pre-history." *Film History* 11,
no. 2 (1999): 204–16.

Hedren, Paul L. "Charles King." In Paul Andrew Hutton, ed., *Soldiers
West: Biographies from the Military Frontier.* Lincoln: University of
Nebraska Press, 1987.

————. "The Contradictory Legacies of Buffalo Bill Cody's First Scalp
for Custer." *Montana: The Magazine of Western History* 55, no. 1 (2005):
16–35.

Hendricks, Gordon. *The Edison Motion Picture Myth.* Berkeley, Calif.:
University of California, 1961.

Higgins, Steven, and Charles Musser, curators. *Edison: The Invention of
the Movies.* DVD set. New York: Museum of Modern Art in cooperation with Library of Congress, 2005.

Hilger, Michael. *The American Indian in Film.* Metuchen, N.J.: Scarecrow Press, 1986.

Hill, John, ed. *Oxford Guide to Film Studies,* Oxford, U.K.: Oxford University Press, 1998.

Hitt, Jim. *The American West from Fiction (1823–1976) into Film (1909–1986).*
Jefferson, N.Car.: McFarland, 1990.

Hoxie, Frederick E., ed. *Talking Back to Civilization: Indian Voices from
the Progressive Era.* Boston: Bedford/St. Martin's, 2001.

Hutton, Paul. "Correct in Every Detail: General Custer in Hollywood."
Montana: The Magazine of Western History 41 (1991): 28–57.

Hyams, Jay. *The Life and Times of the Western Movie.* New York: W. H.
Smith, 1983.

Israel, Paul. *Edison: A Life of Invention.* New York: John Wiley and Sons,
1998.

Jacobs, Lewis. *The Rise of the American Film: A Critical History.* New York:
Columbia University, 1939, 1948, 1967.

Johnson, Virginia W. *The Unregimented General: A Biography of Nelson A.
Miles.* Boston: Houghton Mifflin, 1962.

Johnston, Winifred. "Passing of the 'Wild West.'" *Southwest Review* 21,
no. 1 (1935): 33–51.

Jonnes, Jill. *Eiffel's Tower: And the World's Fair Where Buffalo Bill Beguiled
Paris, the Artists Quarreled, and Thomas Edison Became a Count.* New
York: Viking Penguin, 2009.

————. *Empires of Light: Edison, Tesla, Westinghouse, and the Race to Elec-
trify the World.* New York: Random House, 2003.

Josephson, Matthew. *Edison.* New York: McGraw-Hill, 1959.

Judson, William. "The Movies." In Brooklyn Museum, *Buffalo Bill and the Wild West*. Pittsburgh: University of Pittsburgh, 1981.

Kammen, Michael. *Mystic Chords of Memory: The Transformation of Tradition in American Culture*. New York: Vintage Books, 1991.

Kasson, Joy. *Buffalo Bill's Wild West: Celebrity, Memory, and Popular History*. New York: Hill and Wang, 2000.

Kay, Karyn. "You Can Get a Man with a Gun." *Velvet Light Trap*, no. 8 (1973): 11–13.

Keil, Charlie. *Early American Cinema in Transition: Story, Style, and Filmmaking, 1907–1913*. Madison: University of Wisconsin Press, 2001.

Kensel, W. Hudson. *Pahaska Tepee: Buffalo Bill's Old Hunting Lodge and Hotel, a History, 1901–1946*. Cody, Wyo.: Buffalo Bill Historical Center, 1987.

Kiehn, David. *Broncho Billy and the Essanay Film Company*. Berkeley, Calif.: Farwell Books, 2003.

Kilpatrick, Jacquelyn. *Celluloid Indians: Native Americans and Film*. Lincoln: University of Nebraska Press, 1999.

King, Charles. "Memories of a Busy Life." *Wisconsin Magazine of History* 5, no. 3 (1922): 215–43.

Kinnard, Roy. *Fifty Years of Serial Thrills*. Metuchen, N.J.: Scarecrow Press, 1983.

Knowles, Thomas W., and Joe R. Lansdale, eds. *Wild West Show!* New York: Wings Books, 1994.

Krupicka, Katrina. "Cody and Wanamaker: The Foundation of American Indian Citizenship." *Points West*, Winter, 2003, 24–29.

Lahue, Kalton C. *Continued Next Week: A History of the Moving Picture Serial*. Norman: University of Oklahoma Press, 1964.

———. *Winners of the West: The Sagebrush Heroes of the Silent Screen*. Cranbury, N.J.: A. S. Barnes, 1970.

Larson, Erik. *The Devil in the White City*. New York: Crown Publishers, 2003.

Lentz, Harris M, III. *Feature Films 1960–1969*. Jefferson, N.Car.: McFarland, 2001.

———. *Western and Frontier Film and Television Credits 1903–1995*, Vol. 2. Jefferson, N.Car.: McFarland, 1996.

Lescarboura, Austin C. *Behind the Motion Picture Screen*. New York: Scientific American Publishing, Munn, 1919. http://books.google.com/ebooks/reader?id=dxJ1AAAAMAAJ&printsec=frontcover&output=reader&pg=GBS.PP1.

Lewis, Bernard. *History: Remembered, Recovered, Invented.* Princeton, N.J.: Princeton University Press, 1975.

Lindstrom, Richard. "'Not from the Land Side, but from the Flag Side': Native American Responses to the Wanamaker Expedition of 1913." *Journal of Social History* 30, no. 1 (1996): 209–27.

Maddra, Sam A. *Hostiles? The Lakota Ghost Dance and Buffalo Bill's Wild West.* Norman: University of Oklahoma Press, 2006.

Magill's American Film Guide, Vols. 1–5. Englewood Cliffs, N.J.: Salem Press, 1983.

Manchel, Frank. *Cameras West.* Englewood Cliffs, N.J.: Prentice-Hall, 1971.

Marill, Alvin H. *Movies Made for Television: The Telefeature and the Miniseries 1964–1986.* New York: New York Zoetrope, 1987.

May, Henry. *The End of American Innocence: A Study of the First Years of Our Own Time 1912–1917.* New York: Alfred A. Knopf, 1959.

McGerr, Michael. *A Fierce Discontent: The Rise and Fall of the Progressive Movement in America 1870–1920.* New York: Free Press, 2003.

McGregor, James H. *The Wounded Knee Massacre: From Viewpoint of the Sioux.* Baltimore, Md.: Wirth Brothers, 1940.

Medary, Edward F. "Reminiscences of the Ghost Dance War of 1890–91." *Westerners Brand Book* 3, no. 7 (1946): 45–47, 49–50.

Merritt, Russell. "Dream Visions in Pre-Hollywood Film." In Jay Leyda, ed., *Before Hollywood: Turn of the Century Film from American Archives.* New York: American Federation of the Arts, 1986.

Miles, Nelson A. *Personal Recollections and Observations of General Nelson A. Miles.* Chicago: Werner, 1896; reprint, New York: DaCapo Press, 1969.

———. "Rounding Up the Red Men." In Peter Cozzens, ed., *Eyewitnesses to the Indian Wars, 1865–1890: The Long War for the Northern Plains.* Mechanicsburg, Pa.: Stackpole Books, 2004.

———. *Serving the Republic.* New York: Harper and Sons, 1911.

Miller, Randall M., ed. *The Kaleidoscope Lens: How Hollywood Views Ethnic Groups.* Englewood, N.J.: Ozer, 1980.

Millstead, Thomas. "The Movie the Indians Almost Won." *Westways* 62, no. 12 (1970): 24–26, 55.

Milner, Victor. "Fade Out and Slowly Fade In." *American Cinematographer,* September 1923, 4, 23–24.

Mintz, Steven, and Randy Roberts, eds. *Hollywood's America: United States History through Its Films.* St. James, N.Y.: Brandywine Press, 1993.

Mitchell, Lee Clark. *Westerns: Making the Man in Fiction and Film.* Chicago: University of Chicago Press, 1996.

Mitry, Jean. *The Aesthetics and Psychology of the Cinema.* Trans. Christopher King. Bloomington: Indiana University Press, 2000.

Moorehead, Warren King. *The American Indian in the United States, period 1850–1914.* Andover, Mass.: Andover Press, 1914.

Moses, L. G. *Wild West Shows and the Images of American Indians 1883–1933.* Albuquerque: University of New Mexico Press, 1996.

Mulroy, Kevin, ed. *Western Amerykanski: Polish Poster Art and the Western.* Seattle: University of Washington, 1999.

Munsterberg, Hugo. *The Film: A Psychological Study, the Silent Photoplay in 1916.* New York: D. Appleton, 1916; reprint, New York: Dover, 1970.

Musser, Charles. *Edison in Motion Pictures, 1890–1900: An Annotated Filmography.* Washington, D.C.: Smithsonian Institution Press, 1998.

Musser, Charles, and Carol Nelson. *High Class Moving Pictures.* Princeton, N.J.: Princeton University Press, 1991.

Nasaw, David. *Going Out: The Rise and Fall of Public Amusements.* Cambridge, Mass.: Harvard University Press, 1993.

Nichols, Bill. "History, Myth, and Narrative in Documentary." *Film Quarterly* 41 (Fall 1987): 9–20.

Noble, David W. *The Progressive Mind 1890–1917.* Chicago: Rand McNally, 1970.

Nye, Russel. *The Unembarrassed Muse: The Popular Arts in America.* New York: Dial Press, 1970.

Ostler, Jeffrey. *The Plains Sioux and U. S. Colonialism from Lewis and Clark to Wounded Knee.* Cambridge, U.K.: Cambridge University Press, 2004.

Parish, James Roberts, and Michael R. Pitts. *Great Hollywood Musical Pictures.* Metuchen, N.J.: Scarecrow Press, 1992.

Patterson, Joseph Medill. "The Nickelodeons: The Poor Man's Elementary Course in the Drama." *Saturday Evening Post,* November 23, 1907, 10, 11, 38.

Paul, Andrea I. "Buffalo Bill and Wounded Knee: The Movie." *Nebraska History* 71, no. 4 (1990): 182–90.

Pearce, Roy Harvey. *Savagism and Civilization: The Study of the Indian and the American Mind.* Baltimore: Johns Hopkins University Press, 1953, 1965.

Peterson, Nancy M. "Buffalo Bill, the Movie Maker." *Empire Magazine,* February 27, 1977, 26–33.

————. "Buffalo Bill's Lost Legacy." *American History*, October 2003, 51–67, 80.

Phillips, Ray. *Edison's Kinetoscope and Its Films: A History to 1896*. Westport, Conn.: Greenwood Press, 1997.

Pierce, Edward L. "Recollections as a Source of History." *Massachusetts Historical Society* series 2, 10 (1895–96): 473–90.

Pitts, Michael R., compiler. *Hollywood and American History: A Filmography of Over 250 Motion Pictures Depicting U.S. History*. Jefferson, N.Car.: McFarland, 1984.

————. *Western Movies: A TV and Video Guide to 4200 Genre Films*. Jefferson, N.Car.: McFarland, 1986.

Pratt, George. *Spellbound in Darkness: A History of the Silent Film*. Rochester, N.Y.: University of Rochester, 1966; rev. reprint, Greenwich, Conn.: New York Graphic Society, 1973.

Price, John A. "The Stereotyping of North American Indians in Motion Pictures." In Gretchen Bataille and Charles L. P. Silet, eds., *The Pretend Indians: Images of Native Americans in the Movies*. Ames: Iowa State University Press, 1980.

Radbourne, Allan. "Out of the West, Into the Western." *Wild West*, April 2008, 50–55.

Ramsaye, Terry. *A Million and One Nights: A History of the Motion Picture through 1925*. New York: Simon and Schuster, 1926, 1954.

Ranson, Edward. "Nelson A. Miles as Commanding General, 1895–1903." *Military Affairs*, Winter 1965/66, 179–201.

Reddin, Paul. *Wild West Shows*. Urbana: University of Illinois, 1999.

Rennert, Jack. *100 Posters of Buffalo Bill's Wild West*. New York: Darien House, 1976.

Riley, Glenda. "Annie Oakley." *Montana: The Magazine of Western History* 45, no. 3 (1995): 32–46.

Ringgold, Gene, and Dewitt Bodeen. *The Films of Cecil B. DeMille*. Secaucus, N.J.: Citadel Press, 1969.

Ritchie, Robert C., and Paul Andrew Hutton, eds. *Frontier and Region: Essays in Honor of Martin Ridge*. Albuquerque: University of New Mexico Press, 1997.

Robinson, David. *From Peep Show to Palace: The Birth of American Film*. New York: Columbia University Press, 1996.

Rosa, Joseph G., and Robin May. *Buffalo Bill and His Wild West*. Lawrence: University Press of Kansas, 1989.

Rose, Vicky J. "Lust for the Trail Dust: Cravings for Western Movies." *Roundup Magazine* 17, no. 4 (2010): 23–24.

Rosenstone, Robert A. "Inventing Historical Truth on the Silver Screen." *Cineaste* 29, no. 2 (2004): 29–33.

Russell, Don. "Buffalo Bill—In Action." *Chicago Westerners Brand Book* 19, no, 5 (1962): 33–35, 40.

———. *Campaigning with King: Charles King, Chronicler of the Old Army.* Lincoln: University of Nebraska Press, 1991.

———. "Captain Charles King." *Westerners New York Posse Brand Book* 4, no. 2 (1957): 39–40.

———. *The Lives and Legends of Buffalo Bill.* Norman: University of Oklahoma, 1979.

———. "'My Friend, Buffalo Bill' as told by Gen. Charles King to Don Russell." *Cavalry Journal* 41, no. 173 (1932): 17–20.

———. *The Wild West.* Fort Worth, Tex.: Amon Carter Museum of Western Art, 1970.

Sarf, Wayne Michael. *God Bless You, Buffalo Bill: A Layman's Guide to History and the Western Film.* East Brunswick, N.J.: Associated University Presses, 1983.

Savada, Elias, ed. *American Film Institute Catalog, Film Beginnings 1893–1910.* Metuchen, N.J.: Scarecrow Press, 1995.

Sell, Henry Blackman, and Victor Weybright. *Buffalo Bill and the Wild West.* New York: Oxford University Press, 1955; New York: Signet Key Books, 1959.

Seton, Ernest Thompson. *The Book of Woodcraft.* Garden City, N.J.: Doubleday, Page, 1912.

Shirley, Glenn. *Pawnee Bill: A Biography of Major Gordon W. Lillie.* Albuquerque: University of New Mexico Press, 1958.

Simmon, Scott. *The Invention of the Western Film: A Cultural History of the Genre's First Half-Century.* Cambridge, U.K.: Cambridge University Press, 2003.

Simon, William G., and Louise Spence. "Cowboy Wonderland, History, and Myth: 'It Ain't All That Different Than Real Life.'" *Journal of Film and Video* 47 (Spring-Fall 1995): 67–81.

Sklar, Robert, and Charles Musser, eds. *Resisting Images: Essays on Cinema and History.* Philadelphia: Temple University Press, 1990.

Slide, Anthony. *Aspects of American Film History prior to 1920.* Metuchen, N.J.: Scarecrow Press, 1978.

————. *Early American Cinema.* Lanham, Md.: Scarecrow Press, 1994.

————. *Nitrate Won't Wait: A History of Film Preservation in the United States.* Jefferson, N.Car.: McFarland, 2000.

Slotkin, Richard. *Gunfighter Nation: The Myth of the Frontier in Twentieth-Century America.* New York: HarperCollins, 1992.

————. "Nostalgia and Progress: Theodore Roosevelt's Myth of the Frontier." *American Quarterly* 33, no. 5 (1981): 608–37.

Smith, Andrew Brodie. *Shooting Cowboys and Indians: Silent Western Films, American Culture, and the Birth of Hollywood.* Boulder: University Press of Colorado, 2003.

Smith, Henry Nash. *Virgin Land: The American West as Symbol and Myth.* Cambridge, Mass.: Harvard University Press, 1978.

Sorlin, Pierre. *The Film in History: Restaging the Past.* Totowa, N.J.: Barnes and Noble Books, 1980.

Spurr, Henry C., "The Nickelodeons: A Boon and a Menace." *Case and Comment* 18, no. 10, (1912): 565–73.

Standing Bear, Luther. *My People the Sioux.* Lincoln: University of Nebraska Press, 1975.

Stanfield, Peter. "The Western 1909–14: A Cast of Villains." *Film History* 1, no. 2 (1987): 97–112.

Steckmesser, Kent Ladd. *The Western Hero in History and Legend.* Norman: University of Oklahoma Press, 1965.

Steinbach, Robert H. *A Long March: The Lives of Frank and Alice Baldwin.* Austin: University of Texas Press, 1989.

Steiner, Jesse F. *The Rise of Urban America.* New York: McGraw-Hill, 1933; reprint, New York: Arno Press, 1970.

Stross, Randall. *The Wizard of Menlo Park: How Thomas Alva Edison Invented the Modern World.* New York: Crown, 2007.

Tarbox, Charles. *Lost Films 1895–1917.* Los Angeles: Film Classic Exchange, 1983.

Tate, Alfred O. *Edison's Open Door: The Life Story of Thomas A. Edison, a Great Individualist.* New York: E. P. Dutton, 1938.

Thompson, David. "Movie Violence May Be Harmful." In Roman Espejo, ed., *The Film Industry.* Detroit: Greenhaven Press, 2009.

Trachtenberg, Alan. *Shades of Hiawatha: Staging Indians, Making Americans 1880–1930.* New York: Hill and Wang, 2004.

Tribe, Keith. "History and the Production of Memories." *Screen: Journal of the Society for Education in Film and Television* 18, no. 4 (1977–78): 9–23.

Turner, Frederick Jackson. *The Significance of the Frontier in American History* in *Annual Report of the American Historical Association for the Year 1893*. Washington, D.C.: Government Printing Office, 1894.

Tuska, John. "The American Western Cinema." In Jack Nachbar, ed., *Focus on the Western*, Englewood Cliffs, N.J.: Prentice-Hall, 1974.

Utley, Robert M. *Frontier Regulars: The United States Army and the Indian 1866–1891*. Lincoln, Neb.: Bison Books, 1984.

Utley, Robert M., and Wilcomb E. Washburn. *Indian Wars*. New York: American Heritage Press, 1977, 1987, 2002.

Vermilye, Jerry. *The Films of the Thirties*. Secaucus, N.J.: Citadel Press, 1982.

Walls, Howard Lamarr. *Motion Pictures 1894–1912 Identified from the Records of the United States Copyright Office*. Washington, D.C.: Copyright Office, Library of Congress, 1953.

Walsh, Richard J. *The Making of Buffalo Bill*. Indianapolis: Bobbs-Merrill, 1928; reprint, Cody Family Association, 1978.

Warren, Louis S. *Buffalo Bill's America*. New York: Vintage Books, 2005.

Weltman, Manuel. *Pearl White: The Peerless, Fearless Girl*. New York: A. S. Barnes, 1969.

West, Elliott. "Stories: A Narrative History of the West." *Montana: the Magazine of Western History* 45, no. 3 (1995): 64–76.

Wetmore, Helen Cody. *Buffalo Bill: Last of the Great Scouts*. Stamford, Conn.: Longmeadow Press, 1994.

Wheeler, Richard. *The Honorable Cody*. Santa Fe, N.Mex.: Sunstone Press, 2006.

Whissel, Kristen. "Placing the Spectator on the Scene of History: The Battle Re-enactment at the Turn of the Century, from Buffalo Bill's Wild West to the Early Cinema." *Historical Journal of Film, Radio and Television* 22, no. 3 (2002): 225–43.

White, Richard, and Patricia Nelson Limerick. *The Frontier in American Culture*, ed. James R. Grossman. Berkeley: University of California Press, 1994.

Williamson, Bruce. "Playboy Interview: Robert Altman." *Playboy* 23, no. 8 (1976): 53–58, 62, 160.

Wilson, R. L., with Greg Martin. *Buffalo Bill's Wild West: An American Legend*. New York: Random House, 1998.

Winch, Frank. *Thrilling Lives of Buffalo Bill, Col. Wm. F. Cody, Last of the Great Scouts and Pawnee Bill, Major Gordon W. Lillie, White Chief of the Pawnees*. New York: S. L. Parson, 1911.

Winchester, Juti. "All the West's a Stage: Buffalo Bill, Cody, Wyoming and Western Heritage Presentation, 1846–1917." Unpublished diss., Northern Arizona University, May 1999.

Wooster, Robert. *Nelson A. Miles and the Twilight of the Frontier Army.* Lincoln: University of Nebraska Press, 1993.

Wright, Will. *Six Guns and Society: A Structural Study of the Western.* Berkeley: University of California Press, 1975.

Yellow Robe, Chauncey. "The Indian and the Wild West Show." *Quarterly Journal of the Society of American Indians* 2 (January–March 1914): 39–40.

Yoggy, Gary A., ed. *Back in the Saddle: Essays on Western Film and Television Actors.* Jefferson, N.Car.: McFarland, 1998.

Yost, Nellie Snyder. *Buffalo Bill: His Family, Friends, Fame, Failures, and Fortunes.* Chicago: Swallow Press, 1979.

Index